AUG 10

CH

WINNING
in
TROUBLED
TIMES

WINNING
in
TROUBLED TIMES

GOD'S SOLUTIONS
FOR VICTORY OVER
LIFE'S TOUGHEST
CHALLENGES

DR. CREFLO
DOLLAR

NEW YORK   BOSTON   NASHVILLE

Winning in Troubled Times is dedicated to the partners, friends, and supporters of Creflo Dollar Ministries. Thank you for your prayers and support, as we continue to change lives all over the world. Keep winning!

For everyone born of God overcomes the world.
This is the victory that has overcome the world, even our faith.
—1 John 5:4 (NIV)

CONTENTS

INTRODUCTION

CHRISTIANS ALWAYS WIN

When the United States officially went into recession in December of 2007, I began to notice how Christians were responding to its effects. I was deeply disturbed to find that many believers did not know how to use their faith to win in the midst of troubled times. If that wasn't bad enough, I heard a report that revealed that the divorce rate among Christians was the same as that among unbelievers. Sadly, I came to the conclusion that many Christians simply do not know enough about faith to survive in hard times. As a result, they end up in bad situations because of the pressure they are under. Therefore, they end up suffering along with the rest of the world when trouble comes, and even when times get better.

However, I continue to proclaim, "The kingdom of God never goes through recession, and God is never broke!" Understand that God is never defeated, no matter what is going on in the world. Since God, who is our Source, is never defeated, as Christians, we can never be defeated! In other words, we always win!

I remember the times when I did not know what to do about my finances or how to succeed in my marriage. Not knowing what to do is a miserable state to be in! That is why I am so passionate about God's people gaining understanding of the biblical principles He has revealed to me that have enabled me to live victoriously. When I received a revelation of these things, I began to overcome financial pressures, including huge amounts of debt that kept my wife, Taffi, and me in bondage for years. Having financial burdens can lead to stress and other problems that affect our lives. But God delivered us by empowering us through the knowledge of His Word. He began to lead and guide us to where we are today.

The purpose of this book is to share what God has shown us through studying and teaching His Word. Furthermore, I want to challenge your thinking on how you view prosperity. I want you to ponder and really meditate on the meaning of 3 John 2 (we'll discuss it more below) because you need to *really* believe God will prosper you, even in troubled times.

This book can be used as a reference or as a guide for daily Bible reading. I encourage you to use it in your Bible studies or group discussions concerning everyday issues we all face in life.

THE TRUEST FORM OF PROSPERITY

Third John 2 says, "Beloved, I wish above all things that thou mayest prosper and be in health, even as thy soul prospereth." The word *prosper* originated from the Greek word *euodoó*, which is a parting utterance in the category of words like good-bye, farewell, or bon voyage.[1] So the original word means to successfully reach a destination safe and sound. Therefore, the word has evolved to mean a continuous well-being in every area of life.

This message about prosperity has been greatly attacked over the years because people have been deceived by the enemy. Satan wants to convince us that "all preachers want is our money." Well, I'm not interested in stealing money. I honor and reverence God too much to mess with His people and their money! I am, however, interested in seeing people prosper God's way.

Money is only a part of prosperity. What good is it for us to prosper in our bank accounts and not in our health, relationships, marriages, and families?

True prosperity is being successful in every arena of our lives. It is excelling to the point desired. For example, prospering in my spirit is being born again or having a personal relationship with Jesus Christ. When I prosper in my soul, my thinking, decisions, and emotions are sound and stable. Prospering in my health means I am healthy, free of any ailments or diseases. To prosper the way God wants us to prosper means that we prosper in every way, for He delights in the prosperity of His servants (Psalm 35:27).

So why does God want us to have true prosperity? He wants to show the world that there is profit in serving Him. When we prosper, we can help and serve others. When the church prospers, we are empowered to further the Gospel message around the world. Jesus is coming back for a church without spot or wrinkle. This means He is not coming back for a body of sick, broke, and oppressed believers. He is coming back for a glorious church!

YOU CAN BE WHOLE IN EVERY AREA OF LIFE

Romans 12:2 says, "And be not conformed to this world: but be ye transformed by the renewing of your mind that ye may prove what is that good, and acceptable, and perfect, will of God." There is a difference between true prosperity and false prosperity. The huge difference is this: the blessing of the Lord makes *truly* rich and He adds no *sorrow* with it (Proverbs 10:22). *Rich* in this context means wholeness, nothing missing or broken in our lives.

Many people who have prospered the world's way—through selfishness, greed, and lust—are living in deception. On the surface, it appears they have it all—the dream car, nice job, perfect family, and so on. However, if we look a little closer, we notice that what they have brings them sorrow! The dream home and car may carry notes so heavy they can barely cover them, even with high-paying jobs! They may appear to have the perfect marriage, but we cannot see what takes place behind closed doors.

Others may appear to have the job of their dreams, but what we may not see is the sadness or loneliness deep within. God's way is always perfect. He perfects all things concerning us.

Many people ask me what is the secret to true prosperity. It is simply this: I live according to the Word of God. I trust Him. I trust His system. My trust is not in the world's system, or the government, or anyone else. As you read these pages, I encourage you to place your trust in a loving Father who cannot fail.

Whenever you find yourself battling tough issues or worrying about the chaos that is going on in the world, I want you to pick up this book and realize there is a way out. But that way out is going to require two major changes—a change in the way you think and the way you view the kingdom of God.

Our God always causes us to triumph through Christ Jesus. My prayer for you as you read these pages is that you will find practical knowledge and clear understanding of biblical principles that can be applied to any area of your life for lasting success. Regardless of what you may be facing, how things may seem, or how you may feel, victory in Jesus *is* assured—we always win!

SECTION ONE

WINNING AT WORK AND IN YOUR FINANCES

THE COMBINATION TO
TRUE PROSPERITY

Faith is confidence, trust is a commitment.
Trust says, "No matter what happens, I am going to
believe God."

When I was growing up, my family did not have much financially. Watching my parents struggle to make ends meet created in
me a determination not to live that way for the rest of my life. I developed a burning desire to prosper and help others prosper as well.

Before God called me into ministry, I was frustrated by some
of the traditional religious teachings I heard. Many Christians did
not understand how to apply practically the Word of God to their
everyday lives. As a result, they failed to see His Word manifested
in their lives, and they remained broke, busted, and disgusted.
However, I knew if people were taught how to apply the Word to
their lives, they would prosper. As I pondered this thought, God
spoke to me and said, "That is what I am calling you to do."

I am called to teach people that it is God's will for them to prosper. Please understand that prosperity does not only deal with our
finances but every area of our lives. To prosper means *to excel to the
point desired*. It is making good progress in the pursuit of anything
desirable. Unfortunately, there are some Christians who believe
the word *prosperity* relates only to their finances. But those who
decide to focus only on money will miss the truth of this entire
message. Then there are believers who have knowledge of certain
biblical truths, but they fail to apply their knowledge properly.

For example, only the right combination of numbers will open a locked safe. Likewise, there is a combination of seven steps that will unlock true prosperity.

Biblical laws are established principles that will work for anyone who will get involved with them. Over the years, I have learned certain principles that have changed my life from poverty to abundance. The application of these principles causes abundance to overflow in our lives. When spiritual and natural laws come together, they create a force that rearranges and changes things. Notice, we must combine the spiritual *and* the natural. Most Christians do not receive the promises of God because they neglect to do what needs to be done either in the spiritual or the natural. We cannot go too far to the right or the left. We must have balance.

God wants us to live supernatural lives. *Supernatural* simply means God placing His super on our natural. The problem with some believers is they place all of their attention on the *super* (God's ability) and not enough on their *natural* abilities. I often tell my congregation that we must not be so spiritual that we are no earthly good. And we should not become so natural-minded that we are not spiritually sound. Again, there must be a balance in order to succeed God's way.

God desires for us to prosper and have success. Third John 2 in the Amplified Bible says, "Beloved, I pray that you may prosper in every way and [that your body] may keep well, even as [I know] your soul keeps well and prospers." So, what is the foundation for prosperity? What does it take to win in every area of life? The seven steps that follow will answer these questions.

STEP ONE: UNDERSTAND GOD'S WAY
OF DOING THINGS

It is not enough to wear a Christian T-shirt and proclaim to be a Christian. We must know and understand how God operates to receive what He has for us. If we don't understand the kingdom of God system, true biblical prosperity will not be a reality in our lives. Matthew 6:33 says, "But seek ye first the kingdom of God, and his righteousness; and all these things shall be added unto you."

Additionally, Jesus uses a parable in Mark chapter 4 to illustrate how the kingdom of God system operates. I call this the granddaddy of all parables because if we do not understand this one, we won't understand any of the others. Basically, Jesus uses the parable of the sower to compare the kingdom of God to farming. If you are not familiar with this passage of Scripture, I encourage you to read it until you gain understanding. It will change your life! Here are a few comparisons between farming and the kingdom of God:

- In farming, there is a farmer. In the kingdom of God, you are the sower or farmer.

- A farmer uses seed. In the kingdom of God, the Word is the seed. Therefore, the Bible should not be viewed as a book of rules, but rather a bag of seeds.

- A farmer plants his seed into good ground. In the kingdom of God, our hearts are the ground or soil into which we sow the Word of God.

- In farming, equipment is used in the process of cultivating the seeds. In the kingdom of God, our method of cultivating seeds (the Word) is through speaking faith-filled words.

The root or origin of everything in the kingdom of God is His Word. The kingdom of God, which is God's manufacturing center for life, is located within each of us (see Luke 17:21). The manufacturing center of prosperity requires a sower, sowing the Word. We must plant the Word in our hearts, and the center will produce it. We have to sow our seeds and protect our harvest. Basically, this means once we find a Scripture dealing with an area of concern, such as healing, we must meditate, ponder, and speak the Word until it comes to pass in our lives. Regardless of what it may look like or feel like, we cannot allow anything to seep into our hearts and destroy the Word of God that is planted there.

Keep in mind that lessons that pertain to life and godliness are in the Bible. God's Word, which is Word seed, houses life. The Word has potential to grow the fruit or life on the inside of *us*, once it is planted.

When we refer to sowing a seed, it is common for most believers to automatically think of sowing a financial seed (giving an offering). However, our money seed will not have a future unless we have first planted the Word in our hearts. We must have full acceptance and confidence in the Word that inspires our giving.

For example, Luke 6:38 teaches us to give and it shall be given to us. Therefore, when we give, expecting that specific Word to come to pass, we begin the process of getting the Word in our hearts. And speaking faith-filled words will plant the Word deeply in our hearts. Therefore, expectation and speaking the Word will grow what we are believing to see come to pass in our lives.

STEP TWO: MATURE IN LOVE

The kingdom of God is a kingdom of love. In Matthew 22:37–40, Jesus says, "Thou shalt love the Lord thy God with all thy heart, and with all thy soul, and with all thy mind. This is the first and great commandment. And the second is like unto it, Thou shalt love thy neighbor as thyself. On these two commandments hang all the law and the prophets." If we do not mature in love, we will not see true prosperity.

All the laws that govern prosperity—healing, deliverance, divine protection, financial prosperity—hang on the law of love.

If we refuse to develop in character, forgiveness, and love, we will not receive the kingdom of God prosperity, which is greater than the prosperity the world system offers. When we prosper God's way, there is no sorrow attached to it (Proverbs 10:22).

Being immature in love is equal to being a child spiritually. The Bible says a child will not be able to receive his heritage until he is grown (Galatians 4:1–2). Paul said, *When I was a child, I spoke as a child, understood as a child, and thought as a child, but when I became a man, I put away childish things* (see 1 Corinthians 13:11). Paul was explaining the law of love. In order to be spiritually mature men and women, we have to operate in love. If we refuse to forgive others, we are not mature in love. Kingdom prosperity is always insulated with love. God will not trust a selfish, immature person with wealth or supernatural results.

While money is not the sum total of prosperity, it is an amplifier. It amplifies our current mind-set and condition in life. For example, if a person is selfish, money amplifies selfishness, which can be dangerous. That person can hurt himself as well as others. God will not entrust prosperity to those who are not mature enough to be good stewards over what He has given them.

Immature people often have a wrong attachment to money. In other words, they love money more than they love God and others. We are not supposed to desire money solely to satisfy our own selfish desires. This explains why many Christians have yet to prosper in all areas of life.

So how do we know when we have a wrong attachment to money? The decisions we make determine our level of spiritual maturity. When we allow all our decisions to be driven by our desire for money or selfish gain, we know that we have wrong motives for financial prosperity.

STEP THREE: HAVE PURITY OF HEART

Having a pure heart means we are genuine. There is always a distinction between what is genuine and what is fake. For example, my daughter Jordan bought some perfume while visiting New York. The packaging resembled the real perfume. But when she sprayed it, it smelled awful. It wasn't authentic. Likewise, no matter how sincere or genuine a person may appear on the outside, it is what's on the inside that counts. A mature love walk will always be the distinguishing trait, separating those who have pure hearts from those who do not.

In addition to walking in the love of God, a pure heart is the gateway into the life of the miraculous. It will guarantee unending manifestations in our lives and cause the power of God to flow through us unhindered.

In order to obtain and maintain hearts that are pure before God, we must walk in obedience to Him. Our love for Him and others will purify our hearts. When we have the love of God in our hearts and a desire to be like Jesus on our minds, we are purified (1 John 3:1–3).

STEP FOUR: MEDITATE

Wisdom is divine knowledge that comes to us when we do not know what to do. We acquire wisdom by reading and meditating on the Word of God. For many people, meditation seems spooky, and some associate it with the occult. However, the Bible teaches us to meditate on His Word so that we may be equipped to handle every situation.

Meditation is speaking the Word, considering it, and spending time with it. It involves spending time with Scriptures until revelation and enlightenment come.

After Moses died, God told Joshua to meditate on the Word day and night to observe to do all that is in it (Joshua 1:8). God said by doing so, Joshua would make his way prosperous and learn to deal wisely in his affairs. Meditating on the Word empowers us to attend to all areas of our lives with godly wisdom.

In the early days of my ministry, I used to spend hours praying before a convention or crusade service. I would also fast that day. By the time I got up to preach, I was weak, dizzy, and just plain tired! I knew something was wrong. I prayed and asked God to help me figure it out. He said to me, "I want you to spend your time meditating on the Word before you preach. Spend time in prayer every day. But the most important thing you can do before you preach is meditate on the Scriptures you are going to use in your sermon. I will reveal to you what to say as you study My Word."

When I received this revelation from the Lord, I saw clearly how meditating on the Scriptures would make my way prosperous. As a result of following God's instructions, I am able to receive great revelation knowledge that I am able to share with others.

STEP FIVE: GET SEED

Romans 10:17 says faith comes by hearing the Word of God. In other words, faith comes out of the Word. We have to hear it over and over again until it becomes more real to us than our circumstances. Ultimately, that Word will grow and manifest in our lives.

Additionally, we have to get our speaking involved in the process and have confidence that what we are saying will come to pass. In Matthew 17:20, Jesus says, "For verily I say unto you, If ye have faith as a grain of mustard seed, ye shall say unto this mountain, Remove hence to yonder place; and it shall remove; and nothing shall be impossible unto you." Our faith-filled words are like that grain of mustard seed. It starts small, but once we sow it, it grows.

STEP SIX: APPLY CORRESPONDING ACTION

After the farmer plants his seeds, his work isn't finished. There are actions he must take to ensure his seeds will produce the desired harvest. The same is true for us. What actions do we take once we get the Word planted in our hearts? The Bible teaches that faith without works is dead (James 2:20). The word *works* simply means *action*. Our action must correspond and harmonize with our faith if we are going to see what we are believing to receive from God.

Many believers get into trouble when it comes to choosing the right corresponding action. In most cases, the action they take is a stretch for the level of faith they have developed. For example, when the bills are due but you don't have the money to pay them, you can confess the Word of God concerning your finances, saying, "I believe God has met my needs." However, the wrong corresponding action would be to write checks for all your bills and mail them to your creditors, believing God will put the money in the bank before the checks are cashed!

That example may seem a little outlandish, but there are people who do this and call those bad checks "faith checks." But of course, this action is illegal, and God is not going to support illegal activities! As we confess the Word over our finances, a proper corresponding action would be to write a check for the payoff amount and place it on the dresser until we see the manifestation of the confession.

Below are a few other corresponding actions that are agreeable and suitable as we stay in faith.

Give

We can make a living through our giving. As the saying goes, "What goes around comes around." Actually, we can trace the origin of this statement to the Word of God. Whatever we sow, we also reap (Galatians 6:7). Whenever we give in faith, according to the Word of God, we can expect it to come back to us.

Work

Working is an appropriate corresponding action because we know the Word says if we don't, we don't eat. It is unrealistic for us to think money will fall from the sky. Working gives God an avenue through which He can bless us. As we work our jobs or assignments unto Him, He is faithful to bless us.

Think

God will give us the ability to think of ways to work smarter and more efficiently.

He gives us wisdom when we ask for it. However, we cannot sit down and just wait for something to happen. We have to take action, and thinking in line with God's Word is a correct corresponding action.

Trust

Although it may not appear to be an action, trusting God is a correct and necessary corresponding action. While faith is confidence, trust is a commitment. Trust says, *No matter what happens, I am going to believe God.*

Talk

I cannot place enough emphasis on the power of our words. Death and life are in the power of the tongue (Proverbs 18:21). Instead of speaking negative words that are contrary to the Word of God, we must speak words of life into our circumstances. We have to guard our mouths and be sure we are not contradicting what God has already said about us and our circumstances. Our negative speaking blocks many blessings in our lives. Begin to practice speaking God's Word concerning different areas of your life and watch how your world will change for the better! Call a like-minded friend and just begin speaking the Word about any area of concern in your life.

STEP SEVEN: PRACTICE PATIENCE

Patience is defined as *tolerating a negative situation for a period of time.* However, a biblical definition of patience is *remaining consistently and constantly the same concerning the Word planted in our hearts.* For example, let's say you have planted a particular Word seed for a financial breakthrough. You have the Word in your heart that says God supplies your needs according to His riches in glory through Christ Jesus (Philippians 4:19). You continue to confess that Word despite contradicting situations and circumstances. You continue to say what you believe, even while you are looking at the bills you cannot pay. Then an unexpected bill comes in the mail, and now you are tempted to get depressed because you haven't paid the bills you already have! Despite the situation or how you feel, patience keeps your faith working. Patience says, "I am not going to let the Word of God go—no matter what. I will remain steadfast in spite of what it looks like."

If we are going to win, we must hold on with bulldog tenacity to the Word we have planted. Whenever we allow ourselves to doubt, we have cast away our patience and confidence in the Word. Hebrews 10:35–36 says, "Cast not away therefore your confidence [your faith], which hath great recompence of reward. For ye have need of patience, that, after ye have done the will of God, ye might receive the promise."

WORK IS NOT A DIRTY WORD

2

While saying confessions, praying, and giving are all spiritual laws we must activate to become successful God's way, we cannot ignore the application of natural laws.

ᕲ᳆᷍ Working is a part of life and should be embraced by everyone who wants to achieve success. It is a practical component of success. As a matter of fact, the Bible mentions working approximately seven hundred times! Vince Lombardi once said, "The only place where success comes before work is in the dictionary." Lombardi was known for being one of football's most accomplished and respected coaches of all time. He made winning the Super Bowl a habit, so I am sure he knew a little about hard work and success. Those who have acquired any level of success have sacrificed, studied, and worked hard on their jobs or in their businesses to achieve their success.

However, many people believe they can achieve success without putting in the work. They try any- and everything they think will bring them easy money, such as the lottery, pyramid and get-rich-quick schemes, and even crime. To them, the word *work* is a dirty word. But nothing could be further from the truth.

The Bible says in Proverbs 10:4, "He becometh poor that dealeth with a slack hand: but the hand of the diligent maketh rich." Yes, it is important for us to work diligently. As we can see in this Scripture, people become poor because of their laziness. Just as we can become rich, we can become poor. The choice is ours. This

Scripture is saying that those who work diligently will become rich, while those who are slack in what they do become poor.

Many Christians believe they can simply come to church, give an offering, say a confession or two, and one day they will wake up wealthy. They have adopted what I call a "jackpot mentality." They are waiting on some big event or for God to appear like a genie and grant their wishes. While saying confessions, praying, and giving are all spiritual laws we must activate to become successful God's way, we cannot ignore the application of natural laws.

When Taffi and I were in debt, God spoke to me about the ant. Proverbs 6:6–8 says, "Go to the ant, thou sluggard; consider her ways, and be wise. Which having no guide, overseer, or ruler, provideth her meat in the summer, and gathereth her food in the harvest." In this Scripture, the ant's ways are called wise. So it is wise for us to work hard and store something up for the future to avoid hard times.

We made a commitment to get out of debt, and we knew with that commitment would come hard work. God did not wave a wand or appear in a vision. Instead, His provision for us included our earnings from our hard work, and He blessed what we had. We began to see the *super* added to our *natural*. In the midst of the hard work and commitment, God did move in certain areas of our finances. God honors hard work.

THE MIRACLE OF LIKE SUBSTANCE

God wants to increase us by multiplying what we have. Even with His blessing on our lives, we must give Him something to work with. This is what I call the miracle of like substance. It is when we have something God can multiply, causing us to end up with much more than we originally had.

Jesus demonstrated this principle when He fed a multitude of men, women, and children with five loaves and two fish. Matthew 14:16–20 describes this miracle.

> But Jesus said unto them, They need not depart; give ye them to eat. And they say unto him, We have here but five loaves, and two fishes. He said, Bring them hither to me. And he commanded the multitude to sit down on the grass, and took the five loaves, and the two fishes, and looking up to heaven, he blessed, and brake, and gave the loaves to his disciples, and the disciples to the multitude. And they did all eat, and were filled: and they took up of the fragments that remained twelve baskets full.

First of all, we see that this miracle of multiplication took faith. It took the disciples giving Jesus something to work with. Even though what they had wasn't enough in the natural, they gave it to Jesus anyway. He blessed the food (commanded the supernatural power of God), broke it, and fed the people. It all began with Jesus using what was available. At the end of the meal, not only were the people satisfied, but there was more than enough food left over!

We can apply this principle to our jobs or businesses as well. Regardless of your job title, God can multiply your current salary if you work diligently. When we continue to give tithes and offerings and live by faith, we will experience increase.

WEALTH IS ACQUIRED, NOT GAINED

Ann Landers once said, "Opportunities are usually disguised as hard work, so most people don't recognize them." Working hard at what we do positions us for financial breakthrough. God has given each of us the strength, talent, skill, or ability to earn a living. And for those of us who are born again and know about the covenant of Abraham, He has extended an even greater blessing. Deuteronomy 8:18 in *The Message* says that God "gave you the strength to produce all this wealth so as to confirm the covenant that he promised to your ancestors."

Too often, people look for opportunities to make money without first finding out what the Word has to say about it. Acquiring something is different from just getting it all at once.

Proverbs 13:11 says, "Wealth gotten by vanity shall be diminished: but he that gathereth by labour shall increase." According to this Scripture, the process of attaining wealth involves our money growing over a period of time. While people are waiting on "the big win," they are squandering money that could be used to help them accumulate the wealth they desire. A get-rich-quick mind-set won't produce lasting wealth. In fact, it is responsible for the addictive lifestyle of gambling that is destroying people's lives every day.

Gambling or playing the lottery (the luck system) usually costs individuals much more than is gained. Contrary to what most people think, it does not and will not produce lasting wealth. In fact, it breeds poverty.

GIVING AND WORKING: A COMBINATION FOR SUCCESS

Proverbs 18:16 says, "A man's gift maketh room for him, and bringeth him before great men." For years I have heard this Scripture misinterpreted. When we use the word *gift* here, it is not referring to a calling, a ministry, or a talent. The word *gift* in the Hebrew language is translated "gratuity" or "thanks offering." Therefore, the gift in this Scripture refers to finances. Our money positions us and brings us before people of influence.

I want to explain another Scripture to help clarify the relationship between giving and diligence. Proverbs 22:29 in the

Amplified Bible says, "Do you see a man diligent and skillful in his business? He will stand before kings; he will not stand before obscure men." While Proverbs 18:16 says our giving will position us in life, this Scripture says our diligent work positions us before great men. Both are required. Our giving and working determine our success in life.

The act of giving produces blessings in our lives. However, working provides the way. I often tell people the blessing is not the car, money, house, etc. It is an empowerment from God that makes us successful in every area of our lives. This is how it works: when we believe God for a promotion or financial blessing, He will give us an idea, a concept, power, favor, or an ability that positions us to receive what we want from God. In other words, He gives us hidden wisdom or revelation knowledge.

We may have an empowerment to get wealth but no channel through which that empowerment can operate. Working provides a channel for the material blessings to flow through. When we are unemployed, God's Spirit will lead and guide us to the right job opportunity. Isn't it wonderful to know our job or business gives God an avenue by which He can bring more blessings into our lives? Work is honorable, and God approves of it. He will bless the work of our hands!

Abraham is a good example of someone who received God's blessing on his business. He made his living rearing cattle. Genesis 13:1–2 in the New International Version says, "So Abram went up from Egypt to the Negev, with his wife and everything he had, and Lot went with him. Abram had become very wealthy in livestock and in silver and gold."

Work not only gives us a sense of accomplishment and pride, but it is also honorable before the Lord. God is always working. Jesus said in John 5:17, "My Father worketh hitherto, and I work." God is actively working in conjunction with the prayers and obedience of mankind to bring His purposes to pass on earth. Since we are reflections of Him, we should also have a mind-set that is intent upon working to accomplish His will for our lives, both spiritually and naturally.

OUT OF WORK? DON'T WORRY!

I realize that an economic downturn can cause the loss of employment and force people to take low-paying jobs just to survive. If you are currently unemployed or are looking for a better job, begin to view your job search from a different perspective. Get God involved! Begin to pray about where *He* wants you to work. Make finding a job a job. Get up every morning with the sole purpose of finding a job. Take the eight hours a day you would work on a job and use that time to search for opportunities to go on job interviews.

I know being unemployed or underemployed is stressful. However, I encourage you to use this opportunity to further examine your career choice. Your career or job choice is a decision that will greatly impact your life. Many times people think this is a very trivial decision. They tell themselves, *As long as I am working and getting paid, that's all that matters.* Yet the career you choose does matter, because your job choice can have a lasting effect on your marriage and family. And it can also have an effect on the way you serve God.

Don't make the mistake so many others have made, which is failing to ask God to reveal His purpose for their lives. These are people who have made their own plans, and as they pursue them, they pray and ask God to bless *their* efforts. But that is not how it works. You don't choose your path in life. You *discover* what God wants you to do as you seek Him, and He gives you the wisdom to accomplish it. No matter what career we choose, true success comes when we fulfill the will of God for our lives, by doing what He has called us to do.

SEEK GOD FIRST

Proverbs 10:22 says, "The blessing of the LORD makes a person rich, and he adds no sorrow with it" (NLT). Don't allow yourself to get seduced into a career just because it pays well.

I can remember when I believed, with every fiber of my being, I was going to play professional football. I had it all mapped out. I planned my life according to what I envisioned for my future. I lifted weights, bench-pressed, and rigorously studied football playbooks. I was convinced football was my future. However, in the midst of my dreaming, I never stopped to ask God what *He* wanted me to do.

My dreams were shattered when I got injured. And my football career came to a screeching halt. I was at the lowest point in my life, and that is when I finally humbled myself and began to seek God and His plan for my life. When I discovered His plan and purpose, I eventually obtained everything I ever desired and more. I am convinced that had I become a professional football player, my life still would have been missing something. Nothing compares to being in the will of God!

God's plan for your life will include abundance in every area. But do not despise small beginnings. Even if you have to start at the bottom and wait for the increase in salary, it does not mean you are not in God's will for your life.

Matthew 6:33 says, "But seek (aim at and strive after) first of all His kingdom and His righteousness (His way of doing and being right), and then all these things taken together will be given you besides" (AMP). When you make seeking God your number-one priority, He will lead you into an honorable career that will meet and exceed your needs.

Seeking God is the spiritual aspect of choosing a career. Now I want to give you some natural things to consider.

Begin with Your Values

What is important to you? How do you see this career and how do you value it? You will never be successful doing something you don't want to do. Passion and service are the two fundamental elements to achieving success. Once you find something you would do for free, if given the opportunity, you have located something that can bring great wealth and success into your life.

Locate Your Skills and Talents

There is a distinction between skills and talents. Skills require a certain amount of training for a person to be proficient. Although you may have been trained to do a certain job, that does not mean you will enjoy it. Your natural talent is something you do well and enjoy doing. Take the time to assess your skills and talents and begin looking for jobs in which you have the opportunities to use both.

Identify Your Preferences

Think about the projects you are passionate about. What type of job do you love doing? What do you prefer not to do? Be honest with yourself when answering these questions. Be sure you are true to yourself, fulfilling your heart's desire and not someone else's. You can start by naming tasks you don't like. This may eliminate possible job and career choices. Also, it can bring you a step closer to finding the right job or career.

Experiment

In my opinion, this is one of the most critical things to consider when choosing a career. Find out if the job you would like is actually a good fit for you. Often people think they would like doing a particular job, but once they are actually doing it, they find there are certain tasks involved they did not consider. Be willing to volunteer. Don't allow yourself to be so connected to money that you miss an opportunity to experiment. A volunteer position or an internship can help you see the ins and outs of a certain career.

See the Bigger Picture

Take the time to get a broader perspective of your job duties and the mission of the company or organization. Learn as much as you can about the career you are considering. Learn about the future of the industry or profession.

Opt for Experience First, Money Second

Take advantage of every opportunity to become the best at what you do. Ask yourself, *Which position offers me the best chance of becoming excellent at what I do?* If you want to be paid the best, you've got to learn how to be the best.

Aim for a Job to Which You Can Give 110 Percent Commitment

Most employers have a low tolerance for people who do not give at least 100 percent. They are looking for people who are enthusiastic and productive. People who give 110 percent will gain the attention of management and often position themselves for promotion and increase.

Build Your Lifestyle Around Your Actual Income, Not Your Expectation

This is a practical concept. No matter what you expect to earn in a year or the next five years, it is wise to plan your financial and personal goals around what you presently earn, not what you hope to earn in the future. Do not live above your means because you are expecting a raise. Too often people make that mistake and find themselves in a financial bind.

Invest 5 Percent of Your Time, Energy, and Money in Furthering Your Career

Take the initiative to make yourself more productive by enhancing your knowledge base. Read books, browse the Internet, or take online courses that will allow you to further develop and grow in your field. Also, be sure to check with your employer for continuing education or career advancement classes. Today many employers allow advanced training programs at no cost to the employee.

Be Willing to Change and Adapt

Be flexible. Employers frown upon employees who are rigid and unwilling to open up to new opportunities and adjustments.

These practical steps should help you in your job search. Ask God to give you further direction and insight. If you have a gut feeling that you are making a wrong decision, do not ignore it. Be patient and seek God. He will order your steps to your next assignment and new opportunity for success.

ESTABLISH A GOOD WORK ETHIC

We must be God-conscious at all times. Only then will we know what it means to work for God and not man.

꩜ Our attitude toward our jobs and how we carry out each detail are crucial to achieving success in the workplace. Many become complacent in their jobs, particularly if they have worked for an employer for a long period of time. That lackadaisical approach hurts them because their attitude and the quality of their work determine their overall success. Good work ethics adds value to employees. How we perform our assigned tasks is just as important as choosing the right job or business.

Some of us were fortunate enough to be raised by parents who instilled strong work ethics and values in us, but not everyone has had that experience. As a result, many people lack good work ethics because they simply were not taught how to develop them.

Good work ethics are basically codes of conduct while on the job. They are an issue of character, which is doing what is right because it is right. Arriving at work on time, performing assignments with excellence, having respect for those in authority, and using the time at work wisely are all good work ethics. When we display this level of character at work, we stand out from the crowd. People who have good work ethics are noticed by their employers and are often promoted based on their work ethics alone.

KNOW FOR WHOM YOU WORK

It does not matter what our occupation may be, at the end of the day we must establish within our minds that we are actually working for God. When we work with this mind-set, we are most likely to do a good job because we want to please Him. We will find ourselves doing what is right all of the time instead of only when we think someone is watching. The Bible gives practical wisdom for every area of life, including the area of work. Ephesians 6:5–8 gives practical advice on how we should work. "Servants, be obedient to them that are your masters according to the flesh, with fear and trembling, in singleness of your heart, as unto Christ; Not with eyeservice, as menpleasers; but as the servants of Christ, doing the will of God from the heart; With good will doing service, as to the Lord, and not to men."

These Scriptures make it clear that we must not pretend to be doing our job well simply because others are watching. God looks at our hearts, and He knows the real deal. For example, a child who is told by his parent to sit down and be quiet may appear to be obedient when he takes his seat. But if the child has a bad attitude and flops down in the seat defiantly, he is still standing on the inside. Likewise, many adults hold an inner attitude of rebellion at work, which does not bring honor to God.

Many years ago, I was given a job at the church I attended. My job was to clean the church. Although the job didn't pay well, I carried out my tasks with excellence. I made sure people were impressed when they entered the bathrooms. I took my time, attending to every detail as I cleaned. You may be thinking, *Well, what's so special about that?* I believe that God considered my heart while I was doing that job and began to lead and guide me to the best path for my life, as a result.

We must be God-conscious at all times. Only then will we know what it means to work for God and not man. As we focus on doing a good job for Him, we stay on task and greatly improve the quality of our job performance.

Colossians 3:23 says, "And whatsoever ye do, do it heartily, as to the Lord, and not unto men." When we become aware of the fact that God's eyes are always on us, that He pays close attention to our every move, most of us will think twice about wasting time, loafing, or disrespecting others.

The person who works for God is concerned about how He views his or her performance. Moreover, when we strive to please God in all we do, others will be pleased with our work as well. As Christians, we have the blessing on our lives, and it will spill over into our assignments at work. We are empowered to excel at whatever we have been assigned to do, and we can do it in excellence.

DRESS YOUR MIND FOR WORK

Preparing our minds is necessary before starting any job or task. Attitude is very important. Adjusting our attitudes *before* we get to the workplace positions us and those we encounter for a good day. Often we do not realize it, but the way we carry ourselves at work helps create either a positive environment or a negative one. Our attitudes derive from our inner thoughts and self-talk.

Therefore, we should judge ourselves in this area. We need to ask ourselves each day: *Am I a complainer? Do I have negative things to say about my work environment and the people I work with? Do I contribute to making my workplace positive or am I helping to make it negative?*

Some of you may be thinking, *Well, Brother Dollar, if you knew what I had to go through at work, you wouldn't have anything positive to say either!* But I know I would not contribute to the problem by adding my negative words to the situation. If we continue to speak and think things that promote negativity, it shouldn't be difficult to understand why our experience at work is negative all the time.

We can begin to cultivate a grateful attitude by waking up each morning, thanking God for another day and the opportunity to bring income into our households. God loves it when we work with enthusiasm unto Him.

WRITE IT DOWN

Habakkuk 2:2 says to write the vision and make it plain so that whoever reads it can run with it. Writing our ideas is a great way to remain focused on developing a solid work ethic. When we have our thoughts and directives in writing, we can refer to them daily and stay focused on what needs to be done.

I've found that it is best to take time out to make a list of ways in which I can be effective. It is wise to set aside free time to ask yourself questions that will help any company or organization tremendously: *How can I be a blessing to my employer and make my boss's job easier? Are there systems I can implement to be more efficient and effective at what I do?* To get started, it would be greatly beneficial to identify time wasters and time savers.

In addition to writing workplace objectives, we should be more proactive about improving the quality of our work in the future. For example, ask your immediate supervisor what you can do to improve the quality of your work. Hearing directly from your superiors leaves no room for guessing. Inquiring about your job performance demonstrates that you take your job seriously and are determined to give 100 percent. And even if the feedback isn't positive, receive it as constructive criticism. Then apply those suggestions to make the necessary changes or adjustments. It will pay off!

START EARLY AND LEAVE LATE

Most of us know people who consistently get to work late but are the first ones out the door when their shift is over. These people will always hinder their own progress. Being disrespectful of the employer's time is one of the biggest mistakes people make at work. These people do not understand the importance of arriving to work on time. As an employer, I can tell the difference in productivity when employees decide to come in late and start wrapping up early. Before long, certain tasks are behind schedule.

It bothers me when I see people nonchalantly drift into work five or ten minutes after their shift starts. I understand emergency situations occur from time to time. However, this should not be the norm. Good employees rarely have emergencies, anyway. But when they do, they are sure to call and let their managers know in a timely manner. This shows they value their employer's time and money. Good employees are in demand these days! Employers want to hire people who will work their shifts and, if necessary, stay until the job is done.

LOAFING ON THE JOB

When people loaf on the job, they are basically not doing what they are paid to do. These are the people we see wasting time, talking on the phone, sending text messages, spending time on Facebook, or doing other unproductive things when they should be working. I believe this is a key reason why some people are not promoted and, in some cases, even lose their jobs.

We can be more mindful of our time at work by paying attention to those things that are taking up our time. For example, talking to coworkers can take up a considerable amount of time. Don't get involved in lengthy conversations during the work day. Instead, schedule time during the lunch break to socialize with coworkers. Excessive time spent talking on the company phone, surfing the Internet, and talking with coworkers does not reflect good work ethics.

One strategy we can use to better utilize our time at work is to set aside a block of time each day to check our e-mails and make important phone calls, rather than doing it throughout the day. For example, we may spend fifteen minutes a day checking our e-mails. If so, it may be best to check once in the morning, once in the afternoon, and then right before we leave the office. If we need to make important phone calls, we can do so during breaks. This way, we use our own time, and not the company's time.

BECOMING INDISPENSABLE

As an employer, I want to encourage you to strive to be the type of employee that any employer simply cannot afford to lose. When you build the type of work ethics that display godly character and the love of God, you become indispensable to your employer.

While diligent hard work is essential to seeing success in our lives, there are some specifics we need to consider regarding the *way* we work.

Here are some things you can do to ensure you are valued by your company:

1. Smile!

2. Try new, creative things.

3. Find more effective and efficient ways to do your job.

4. Arrive early and stay late.

5. Treat your company as if it were your own.

Companies are looking for creative individuals they can count on to help them achieve their objectives with excellence. Be that kind of employee, and promotion will be right around the corner!

APPLYING PRACTICAL FINANCIAL PRINCIPLES

Sacrifices must be made in order to get out of a bad financial situation. And while the Lord will do some supernatural things to help, there is a part in the process we must play.

So many people look at my success and totally disregard the hard work, discipline, and diligence it took for me to be where I am today. They do not understand that Taffi and I had to make some hard decisions and even harder sacrifices. However, I believe the most important decision we made was to commit to making the Word of God our final authority. That decision took us from one level to the next.

Now that we have established a foundation for true prosperity, it is time to take it to the next level. I want to focus on the practical or natural side of financial prosperity and give simple steps to gain and maintain financial freedom, even during troubled times. Proverbs 24:3–4 says, "Through wisdom a house is built, and by understanding it is established; by knowledge the rooms are filled with all precious and pleasant riches" (NKJV). God's wisdom moved us to a better place financially. Many times, the issue is not that we do not have enough money, but that perhaps we are mishandling the finances we have. I am convinced that as Christian people, we would see great results in our finances if we would create a budget and stick to it.

We should never view budgeting as tedious and unnecessary.

Even the smallest of money woes can get out of hand if left unchecked. I like the way Benjamin Franklin said it: "Beware of little expenses. A small leak will sink a great ship." Many people dread the process of developing a plan for their finances because it usually means they will have to discipline themselves where spending is concerned. However, the Word of God actually has a lot to say about budgeting and dealing wisely with our resources.

A budget gives a clear picture of where we are financially. It also gives guidelines so we can achieve the financial status we desire. I remember having to learn the importance of a budget when Taffi and I bought our first home.

One day, I came home and realized we did not own anything in our house! Everything we had was bought on credit—the bed, the furniture, the refrigerator, and the car. Nothing belonged to us, and we did not have any financial safety net in case something happened to either one of us. Our income was not very impressive and our debt-to-income ratio was overwhelming. We were almost $100,000 in debt and desperately needed a way out.

I sat down and made a list of our assets and liabilities. Unfortunately, we had no assets. We had nothing but liabilities. In addition, I identified that I was spending more money than I was actually bringing home! I decided to examine my finances to see where my money was going. I discovered it was time to initiate a plan to get my family out of this situation.

I will never forget my first step. I sat on the edge of the sofa, looked up toward heaven, and said, "God help me!" I had to recognize and acknowledge that I would not be able to get out of this situation without God's help. It wasn't long before negative thoughts began to crowd my mind. I began thinking, *You'll never be able to do this. Getting out of debt is going to take a long time. You're not going to be able to enjoy life anytime soon.* Despite those negative thoughts, I decided to press on and do whatever was necessary to get out of that situation.

God gave me the wisdom I needed to turn things around. I

created a budget and started learning rapid debt-reduction strategies. Additionally, we stopped using credit cards. If we couldn't purchase the item with cash, we just did without it. These sacrifices were necessary in order for us to make progress.

I also decided we needed to increase our incomes. So, Taffi and I worked more hours and began to make lifestyle changes. We eliminated entertainment and other luxuries for a while so that we could put our extra money toward paying off bills. Additionally, we planned our meals in advance and only went to the grocery store with a list. We purchased gas on Sunday night so it would last for the week. Because of the practical things we did, we began to see the light at the end of a very dark tunnel.

We set up a debt-reduction plan and tackled our smallest debts first. Once those were paid off, we used that money to pay off the larger balances. Within six months, we paid off the credit cards. After paying them off, we avoided the temptation to use them by keeping them locked away and continued paying off our remaining debt. We applied the money we had used to pay off the credit cards to pay off the car. Once the car was paid for, we put that money toward paying off our mortgage. Although it wasn't easy, we accomplished our goal. We became debt free.

Sacrifices must be made in order to get out of a bad financial situation. And while the Lord will do some supernatural things to help, there is a part in the process we must play. Taffi and I were willing to do without certain luxuries and apply certain disciplines in order to live a good, stress-free life. It all began with us creating a budget and sticking to it.

WHAT IS A BUDGET?

A budget is a list of all planned expenses and revenues. It is an important economic concept and gives us a financial picture of where we are and where we want to be financially. With a budget, we decide how much to spend on bills, necessities, debt, entertainment, and other areas. We also decide what the difference is between what we need and what we want. It helps us establish our financial priorities and monitor our progress.

Many people are living paycheck to paycheck. This type of lifestyle is proof that there is a need to scrutinize finances and find ways to cut back. Having a budget will help us do just that, while increasing savings and freeing up money for investments.

The thought of living on a budget is a scary concept to some people, but it is actually a biblical principle. When we do not have a budget, it is easy to lose control of our financial goals. Proverbs 22:3 says, "A prudent *man* foresees evil and hides himself, but the simple pass on and are punished" (NKJV). No matter how much money a person makes, wise financial management is a necessity. Spending, saving, and investing are essential elements in money management, and a budget can help us deal wisely in these areas.

A wise man (or woman) considers the cost before embarking on an undertaking. In Luke 14:28, Jesus spoke on the importance of budgeting. "For which of you, intending to build a tower, sitteth not down first, and counteth the cost, whether he have sufficient to finish it?" This is just what budgeting is—counting the cost, analyzing our expenses, and projecting our financial future based on what we can do with the money we currently have.

CREATING A PERSONAL OR FAMILY BUDGET

In a personal or family budget, all sources of income are identified, and expenses are planned with the intent of matching the outgoing to the incoming funds. The important thing to remember is, we should never have more flowing out than we have coming in. When we are spending more than we earn, we are setting ourselves up for hard times.

Financial planning is a dynamic process that requires regular monitoring and reevaluation. Proverbs 27:23–24 says, "Be diligent to know the state of your flocks, *and* attend to your herds" (NKJV). We should constantly keep track of our money and make adjustments where needed to make sure our inflow and outgo remain consistent. In essence, financial planning involves five steps.

Step One: Assessment

Your personal finances can be assessed by compiling simplified versions of financial balance sheets and income statements. A personal balance sheet lists the values of all your personal assets (car, house, clothes, investments, bank accounts) along with your personal liabilities (credit card debt, bank or student loans, mortgage). You also need to create a personal cash flow statement that lists personal income and expenses. Categorize your expenses as fixed or flexible. Fixed expenses are those we incur on a regular basis. Examples include loan payments, telephone bills, monthly office expenses, utilities, car insurance, rent, and mortgage. Flexible expenses can be adjusted or eliminated. These include luxury items such as expensive clothes, unnecessary personal items, visits to salons for hair appointments, manicures and pedicures, etc.

Step Two: Setting Goals

Setting financial goals helps direct your financial planning. It is critical that you set definite, clear goals, and stay focused on them. Some examples of goal-setting are: to buy a house in three years, paying a monthly mortgage servicing cost that is no more than 25 percent of your gross income, or to retire at age sixty-five with a personal net worth of $600,000. Setting goals gives you something to work toward and keeps you motivated to stay on top of your finances.

Step Three: Creating a Plan

I cannot emphasize enough the importance of having a plan. A
financial plan details how to accomplish your goals. It could, for
example, reduce unnecessary expenses, increase your income, or
make allowances for investments. When we fail to plan, we plan
to fail.

Step Four: Execution

Execution of one's financial plan often requires discipline and per-
severance. It is probably one of the most difficult parts of the process. Sticking to your budget is critical. Having a person who will
hold you financially accountable is important. It is not uncommon for people to obtain assistance from professionals such as
certified public accountants (CPAs), financial planners, invest-
ment advisors, and lawyers. If you feel you need more detailed
assistance, and your budget allows for such services, do not hesi-
tate to secure them. If you cannot get a personal accountant, find
a financially responsible, trusted friend or loved one. Let the individual know what you are doing and give him or her permission
to check on your progress. Discuss your budget and the areas in
which you would like to see improvement.

Step Five: Monitoring and Reassessment

As time passes, your personal financial plan must be monitored
for possible adjustments or reassessments. Changes in your
income can affect your budget. For example, if you experience a
decrease in your finances due to job transitions or other setbacks,
you may have to tighten your budget even more. On the other
hand, if you experience a financial increase, it may give you some
leverage and room to do more with your money.

THE LAW OF SAVING, PLANNING, AND ANTICIPATING POTENTIAL SETBACKS

There is a wealth of information in the Word of God on discipline, diligence, and wisdom. These three characteristics lead to success. In fact, I have not known one successful person who did not possess these qualities. Additionally, saving money, investing, planning ahead, and anticipating unexpected situations are disciplines that must be developed in order to prevent setbacks. A person who plans is a person who sets the course for his or her success. When we prepare ourselves ahead of time and lay out exactly how we will accomplish a particular task, we are more likely to carry it out and reach our goal. In life, unexpected situations are almost a guarantee. However, when we prepare for the unexpected, we will not be in desperate need of a miracle on a regular basis.

Planning ahead and anticipating unexpected situations are disciplines that must be developed in order to achieve financial success. Many of us were not taught these disciplines, and I know how hard it is to change bad spending habits. It will definitely require work. However, getting back on track financially is worth the work. Also, when we begin to save our money, we must avoid the temptation to dip into our savings. Again, this will take discipline and practice if you want to experience financial growth and security.

A BIBLICAL PERSPECTIVE ON SAVING

Our quest to become disciplined in the area of saving requires more than willpower. It also takes Word power! God's Word on finances will renew our minds and equip us to become proficient in money matters. Although some of the changes require great (and often uncomfortable) sacrifices, we have to make a quality decision to do what we need to do. For example, if you have developed a habit of spending your money unwisely or you allow your emotions to govern your spending, you will have to patiently tackle those bad habits because these established patterns will not go away overnight. The good news is, the wisdom you will gain from the Scriptures will show you how to become disciplined in managing your finances.

The spiritual aspect of saving is evident in the Scriptures. As we've seen, Proverbs 6:6–8 in the Amplified Bible says, "Go to the ant, you sluggard; consider her ways, and be wise! —which, having no chief, overseer, or ruler, provides her food in the summer, and gathers her supplies in the harvest."

This principle of gathering is a characteristic of the ant that prepares for the coming season by stocking up on what it needs before the time comes. The Word says that when we take a lesson from this creature and follow its ways, we are wise.

Proverbs 30:24–25 says, "There are four things which are little on the earth, but they are exceedingly wise: The ants are a people not strong, yet they lay up their food in the summer" (AMP). Obviously God wants His people to take notice of and emulate the wisdom of the ant. Saving is preparing for the future and whenever hard times come. Then we will always have more than enough to do what needs to be done.

Another benefit of saving and planning ahead is that they give us the ability to leave an inheritance for our children and grandchildren. When we do this, we fulfill the Word of God that says, "A good man leaves an inheritance to his children's children" (Proverbs 13:22 NASB). An inheritance does not just come by osmosis. It takes meticulous planning, wisdom, discipline, and savings to reach the goal. God will provide the resources, but we must be good stewards over them and manage them properly.

WAYS TO SAVE

Being frugal demonstrates financial discipline and helps us increase our assets. I believe it is one of the most important qualities we can have as stewards over the finances God has entrusted to us. Begin to shop smart and spend less. Just because something is available does not mean we have to have it. Being frugal helps us develop temperance where our spending is concerned. Here are a few money-saving suggestions:

- Recognize the difference between needs and wants. Focus on spending money primarily on your needs.

- Open a savings account and, after tithing, pay yourself first.

- Eliminate waste. Use everything to its full potential.

- Recycle and reuse study materials such as pencils, pens, and paper.

- Make plans based on your budget, and make sure that all your responsibilities are met before recreation.

- Do not allow others' spending habits to influence yours.

- Shop smart when buying groceries and household items. Have a list when you go shopping and stick to it. Plan your meals ahead of time and buy only the necessities. Use coupons, shop during sales, and stock up on discounted non-perishable items. Find wholesale grocery stores where you can buy products in bulk.

- Shop smart when buying clothes. Do not pay full retail prices. Shop at thrift stores, consignment shops, and clearance racks. Buy off-season to save money.

- Be selective about long-distance options or call packages that include caller ID, call-waiting, and voice mail. It may be best to get a manual answering machine and use calling cards to make long distance calls.

- Cut down on magazine subscriptions.

Learning how to manage your money will affect your current situation and your future. So ask God to show you more ways to save money and live a more frugal lifestyle. Check with Him before going shopping and pay attention to His voice whenever you make purchases. Acknowledge God in all your ways and He will direct your path.

Proverbs 19:21 in the Amplified Bible says, "Many plans are in a man's mind, but it is the Lord's purpose for him that will stand." Part of God's counsel is the wisdom of a budget. Don't despise this valuable financial management tool. It is designed to help you reach your goals. Make sure it is accessible to you. Keep it on your computer, and print out a copy so you can refer to it quickly. Place the copy in a notebook that you keep with you at all times.

Whether you are trying to get out of debt or just trying to get a handle on out-of-control spending, creating a budget is sure to get you headed in the right direction.

For more information on financial management and budgeting, you can visit these websites*:

- smartmoney.com/PF/

- kiplinger.com

- bankrate.com

- betterbudgeting.com

- HSH.com

* As of press time these websites were functional.

TRIUMPHING 5 OVER DEBT

The first and most important step in God's
supernatural war against debt is for us to remain in the
circle of love. Our ability to love God's way is critical
to our debt deliverance.

Years ago, I taught a message entitled "The Law of Supernatural Debt Release Versus the Law of Intelligent Debt Management." During the message, I asked everyone who was currently
in debt to stand. Nearly 100 percent of the congregation stood up!
At that moment, it was very clear to me why God had led me to
teach on this critical and very sensitive topic. I had to fight back
tears because I was overwhelmed to see how many believers were
in bondage as a result of debt. I knew I had to help God's people
and teach them the law of supernatural debt release.

A *law* is an established principle that will work the same way,
every time, for whoever will put the principle into operation. For
example, gravity is a law. Because of gravity, when we drop an
object it will always fall down instead of floating up.

While gravity is a natural law, there are also spiritual laws. The
law of supernatural debt release is a spiritual law. When we put
this law into operation, it will work for us, regardless of who we
are or where we come from. This is the reason Christians who live
their lives according to the Word of God are more equipped to deal
with debt than non-Christians. We have more weapons available
to us to deal with debt than the person who does not know God's

principles or how they operate. Unbelievers cannot understand it, but we as Christians have to take hold of the arsenal that God has made available to us and use it to get out of the debt trap.

I believe there is an evil, demonic spirit behind debt that is assigned to keep people in financial bondage. The enemy knows that if all our money is signed over to creditors, it will be difficult for us to freely give into the kingdom of God. However, the enemy cannot *make* us do anything we do not want to do. He cannot make us use our credit cards or spend our money unwisely. He can *only* make suggestions. We yield to those suggestions when we give in to the temptation to gain immediate gratification by using our credit cards to fulfill our lustful desires. This opens the door to the spirit of debt, which has the potential to ruin our lives.

The Bible says in Isaiah 50:7, "For the Lord GOD will help me; therefore shall I not be confounded: therefore have I set my face like a flint, and I know that I shall not be ashamed." Some of us have so much debt only God can help us get out! The good news is, God is not limited. He is equipped and willing to help us get out of debt.

THE DEBT CYCLE

There are people who live a majority of their lives making purchases with borrowed money. For these people, debt is a lifestyle. Everything from their televisions to the furniture they sit on is all purchased with credit. I know because I used to be one of those people.

Debt is a huge problem! I will give several reasons why. First, it promotes discontentment. When we constantly buy on credit, we end up being miserable. There will always be a lack of ownership, as well as the uncomfortable feeling of knowing that a ball and chain is attached to the luxury item purchased on credit. We cannot fully enjoy what we have until it is paid off.

When we constantly charge items to our credit cards, using borrowed money, we activate a vicious cycle. Once we get in the habit of buying goods and services this way, it becomes addictive. We can easily find ourselves in a state of depression because of a deepening debt cycle.

Additionally, when we purchase merchandise on credit, we make arrogant presumptions about the future. Unfortunately, life can bring unforeseen circumstances and situations. Setbacks can arise, causing our finances to be redirected. As a result, we can easily get behind in making payments. Whenever we use credit to pay for things, we must keep in mind that we have obligated our future prosperity to paying debt. Before we get into debt, we should consider the impact it will have on our future finances.

Presuming we will have the money to pay our debts sets us up for problems and keeps us trapped in bad spending habits. Many people who do this continue to rationalize their actions, refusing to see the bigger picture.

Another reason debt is such a huge problem is that it requires that we transfer our future wealth to our creditors. Instead of placing our money in high-interest savings accounts or giving to advance the kingdom of God, our hard-earned money is tied to a creditor.

Finally, debt limits our options or eliminates them altogether. When we have a lot of bad debt, it may be more difficult to qualify for bigger purchases like a home, or other important investments.

IT'S TIME TO GET ANGRY

Debt binds many people to jobs and careers they hate. Many even have to take on additional jobs to keep up with their payments. The stress of it all eventually begins to take its toll on people mentally, emotionally, physically, and even spiritually.

If you are in debt, don't beat yourself up about it. Recognize where you made mistakes, repent, and decide right now to change your financial course! Place credit cards in a place where you cannot easily access them and commit to only use cash to purchase things. God will assist you when you do your part.

Christians have been given absolute authority over the works of Satan, and while he is not responsible for the choices we make, he *is* responsible for setting up situations and circumstances that trap us. He plays on our selfish desires and weaknesses to get us to take his bait. It is up to us to recognize his traps and avoid them. The Word of God, the Holy Spirit, and our ability to make quality decisions are our weapons against him.

God does not want to see His children struggling. He will cancel our debts when we activate spiritual principles and do our part in the natural realm. There are numerous examples in the Bible in which God canceled debt. As with any move of God, our freedom from debt requires that we gain practical understanding of our individual roles in the process.

The question is: How angry are we about debt? How willing are we to use violent faith in order to break the debt cycle in our lives? Drastic times call for drastic measures. We must tackle debt and financial lack with the same intensity Jesus displayed when He turned over the tables of the money changers in the temple (Matthew 21:12–13).

God is not a respecter of persons, but He is a respecter of faith. We will not get the job done simply hoping and praying to be debt free. We must have faith in God's ability to bring us out. What He's done for others, He can and will do for us if we believe. Second Kings 6:1–7 gives the account of a borrowed axe head that the Lord caused to float. Here we see the miracle of supernatural debt cancellation.

And the sons of the prophets said unto Elisha, Behold now, the place where we dwell with thee is too strait for us. Let us go, we pray thee, unto Jordan, and take thence every man a beam, and let us make us a place there, where we may dwell. And he answered, Go ye. And one said, Be content, I pray thee, and go with thy servants. And he answered, I will go. So he went with them. And when they came to Jordan, they cut down wood. But as one was felling a beam, the axe head fell into the water: and he cried, and said, Alas, master! For it was borrowed. And the man of God said, Where fell it? And he shewed him the place. And he cut down a stick, and cast it in thither; and the iron did swim. Therefore said he, Take it up to thee. And he put out his hand, and took it.

In this passage of Scripture, God responded by giving His prophet the supernatural ability to perform a debt-releasing miracle. He will do the same for us today. Hebrews 13:8 declares that Jesus Christ is the same yesterday, today, and forever.

GOD'S DEBT-RELEASE PLAN

Step One: Act in Love

The first and most important step in God's supernatural war against debt is for us to remain in the circle of love. Our ability to love God's way is critical to our debt deliverance.

Romans 13:8 teaches us to owe no man anything but unconditional love. The debt to love people is required of every Christian. We should judge ourselves daily where our love walk is concerned. If someone is standing on God's Word for financial breakthrough but has not seen any results, the blockage could be the result of his or her inability to operate in love. We must ask ourselves, *To whom do I owe the debt of love and have not paid it? Is unforgiveness, strife, or past hurt keeping me from loving others the way God commands?* If so, it is time to deal with these issues and get them resolved. God will not allow His supernatural power to flow through our lives if we refuse to love. When we give the gift of love, we can receive the Father's love in the form of supernatural debt cancellation and provision in other areas of our lives as well.

Step Two: Declare God's Word over Your Finances

Once our love foundation is secure, we can begin to receive the promises of God. The Word says when you decree a thing, it is established (Job 22:28). A *decree* is *an authoritative order or established judgment*. When we open our mouths and declare what God has said regarding our finances, we activate the forces of heaven to go to work on our behalf. Therefore, the second step in the supernatural war against debt is to make an announcement against the devil concerning our financial freedom. It is our job to release the power of God to break the power of the spirit behind debt by decreeing that we are released from debt's grip, according to God's Word (Deuteronomy 15:1–4).

Step Three: Bind the Enemy

The third step of the supernatural war against debt is to bind the enemy. This is where a lot of people miss it because they do not understand the importance of binding the enemy.

Believe it or not, demons *do* exist. In fact, there are specific demonic forces assigned to destroy every area of our lives, including our finances. The Bible says we do not wrestle against flesh and blood, but against principalities, powers, rulers of darkness, and spiritual wickedness in high places (Ephesians 6:12). Therefore, the knowledge of the battle set against us will help us effectively arm ourselves with God's Word. Part of our power over the enemy is knowing we are fighting him. We need to know who he is, his tactics, and who we are in Christ.

In Matthew 12:28–29, Jesus expounded upon a key aspect of

spiritual warfare. "But if I cast out devils by the Spirit of God, then the kingdom of God is come unto you. Or else how can one enter into a strong man's house, and spoil his goods, except he first bind the strong man? And then he will spoil his house." We *must* bind the enemy, or as this Scripture describes him, "the strong man," so we can make progress in our war against debt. When we immobilize the enemy by binding him, we have the ability to move forward financially. Therefore, our prayer time should specifically include this aspect of debt deliverance.

Step Four: Apply Violent Faith

Step four in God's war plan on debt is applying violent faith to our financial situations. Violent faith involves building our faith by becoming intense regarding making our confessions, meditating on the Word, listening to CDs, or watching DVDs that contain the Word pertaining to our area of need. We do these things with intensity until we can see the tearing down of spiritual strongholds.

Violent faith is simply a disciplined refusal to take our minds off the Word. We confess the Word with a frequency and intensity that is unmatched. Being violent in the Spirit realm isn't confessing Scriptures once or twice a week and expecting magical results. It takes much more than that to see accelerated results.

When I was diagnosed with prostate cancer, I knew my life was on the line. Therefore, I acknowledged within myself that the disease was working twenty-four hours a day to kill me. I didn't have time to decide whether I was going to believe God's Word or not. I had to take authority over the situation and begin violently increasing my faith for healing.

For several days, I stayed in my room spending time confessing God's Word and playing healing Scriptures at night while I slept, until my spirit was so saturated with God's Word on healing that faith was rising up, overflowing into my mind and body.

The doctor's report had no choice but to line up with the Word because I became violent with my faith! I pounded the mountain of sickness with God's Word, and it had to move!

This is the same stance we must take when it comes to debt. Real freedom requires violence—a force stronger than what is against us. Like disease, debt works twenty-four hours a day to keep us in bondage. Interest is constantly accumulating, making balances grow. We can't afford not to bombard our debt with the Word of God on a consistent basis. That may mean making confessions every hour on the hour until a debt cancellation consciousness is built to the extent that manifestation *has* to take place.

Step Five: Forgive Yourself

The fifth step in God's war plan against debt is forgetting past debts. In order to move forward, we must let go of the condemnation from making bad financial decisions and mistakes. Philippians 3:13–14 says, "Brethren, I count not myself to have apprehended: but this one thing I do, forgetting those things which are behind, and reaching forth unto those things which are before, I press toward the mark for the prize of the high calling of God in Christ Jesus."

If Paul had dwelled on his past mistakes, he never would have embraced God's destiny for his life. The condemnation of his past would have kept him stuck. We must get beyond the bad decisions we have made. Forgetting past debt does not mean we neglect the debts by not paying them. It simply means we press forward despite the mistakes we have made. Worrying over or giving too much attention to our past mistakes causes us to lose the momentum to press forward. In addition, it causes us to doubt God and get into self-condemnation.

Isaiah 43:18–19 says, "Remember ye not the former things, neither consider the things of old. Behold, I will do a new thing; now it shall spring forth; shall ye not know it? I will even make a way in the wilderness, and rivers in the desert." It does not matter how bad our financial mistakes are; we must believe God is willing and able to restore us. He is not standing over us waiting to punish us because we made a mess of our finances. We must believe His love for us and trust that He can and will turn our situations around.

Once we make a quality decision to forget past debts, it's time to press in on the promise of debt cancellation. *Pressing in* means we intensely focus on the spiritual *and* natural aspects of debt cancellation, while being consistent in doing our part.

DEBT CANCELLATION IS GOD'S WILL

We know that 3 John 2 tells us that God's desire is for us to prosper and be in good health. True prosperity begins in our souls, which consist of our minds, wills, and emotions. Being financially unhealthy starts with our thinking and transfers to our actions. If we have a poverty mentality, coupled with a lack of understanding about how to govern our finances according to God's Word, we will continually find ourselves in compromising situations.

In the process of debt cancellation, it is vital to study God's Word so it can renew our minds as we discover what He has to say about our finances. The Word of God is the starting point. As we study the Word, He will speak a Word to us concerning our problems. In other words, God will speak the resolution.

We must find Scriptures on debt cancellation and begin meditating on them. This process enables us to become established in God's Word, which builds our faith. For example, if you have a large amount of debt and are believing God for supernatural debt cancellation, begin speaking to that mountain of debt and command it to be removed in Jesus' name (Mark 11:23). Believe you have received what you have prayed for and continue to stand on God's Word even when it seems as if nothing is happening.

Remember, in addition to doing the spiritual, there is work to be done in the natural as well. Many times, people focus entirely on the spiritual application and completely ignore the practical application of debt release. Discipline, knowledge, and hard work are all necessary to tackle the natural, practical component of debt cancellation.

In the natural, we must realize that our debt *must* be paid back. While there are supernatural means of getting rid of debt, we must not avoid paying someone a debt we owe simply because we are waiting for a miracle to take place. The miracle could come in the form of extra money that can be applied to the debt. Be sure to operate in integrity while paying off your debts. Be consistent and make regular payments to creditors and keep the lines of communication open.

Do your best to get your finances under control and allow God to do the rest. When we initiate the process, He will get involved. However, don't worry about how God is going to cancel your debt or increase you financially. Just know that the biggest testimonies come from people who made the effort to become better stewards over their money. As a result, God honored their efforts and opened doors that allowed them to attain the necessary finances to become debt free. He'll do the same for you.

Also, we must pay attention to the opportunities we receive. God may provide ways we can generate income to help remove debt. Understand, we cannot be so "spiritually deep" that we miss a God-given opportunity. As we stand on God's Word and confess the Scriptures, God blesses us with opportunities to make more money through a business idea, side job, or personal project that He lays on our hearts. These are the natural channels in which He funnels His resources to us.

One of the ways we can release our faith for debt cancellation is by activating God's system of seedtime and harvest. I know from experience that God will bless us when we bless others. I have found that one of the surest ways to get out of debt is by giving financially to someone else who is struggling with debt. In addition, giving financially to anointed prosperous men and women of God will enable us to partake of the same financial blessing that is on their lives. Also, giving tithes and offerings are principles that always cause us to reap a harvest (Genesis 8:22; Malachi 3:8–12; 2 Corinthians 9:6–8; Luke 6:38). God's Word promises it.

God's wisdom is available to any person who desires it. All we have to do is ask. He wants us to live above this world system of finances. However, we are going to require His wisdom to successfully navigate through the world's way of doing things. Debt doesn't have to rule our lives. Instead, we can rule our finances and be in control of our spending. We should strive to be lenders, not borrowers, so that we can be a blessing to others. This can become a reality when we triumph over debt and begin to accumulate the wealth God desires us to have.

SECTION TWO

WINNING IN RELATIONSHIPS

BUILDING FRIENDSHIPS

True friends encourage one another in the things of God. They continue to support one another as they strive to live a life that is in line with the Word.

༺༻ If you're wondering why a book on winning in challenging times includes so many nonfinancial chapters, starting with this one on friendships, it's because relationships, emotions, and addictive behaviors are at the root of most of our money problems. Applying spiritual principles to these areas of our lives will make it possible to successfully apply the work and finance principles of the previous chapters. Think of it in medical terms. Sometimes a doctor can't treat the presenting illness until we make some lifestyle changes. For example, people can't undergo hip-replacement surgery that will help them walk, even run, without pain, before they reach their proper weight and blood pressure. It's the same with winning in life. We're whole beings, created by God. Applying God's principles to our relationships, emotions, and behavior is part of winning financially and being a conqueror, even in the most troubled times.

Do you know who your true friends really are? The people we call "friend" say a lot about us. There are many different definitions and opinions about who a friend truly is, but most of us would agree that a friend is someone we love and trust. According to *Merriam-Webster's Collegiate Dictionary*, a friend is "one attached to another by affection or esteem." A friend is more than just someone we hang out with once in a while, or someone we briefly speak to from time to time. Thomas Jefferson once said, "Friendship is precious, not only in the shade, but in the sunshine of life." Whether we're experiencing life's sunshine or its storms, friends are a very important part of our lives.

What does the Word of God have to say about friendship? Proverbs 17:17 says, "A friend loveth at all times, and a brother is born for adversity." The right friends can be a blessing and the wrong friends can be a curse. If we have the right friends in our lives, they will empower us to succeed. The wrong friends will ultimately cause us to fail.

The word *friend* first appeared in the Bible when God established a covenant with Abraham. A covenant is a promise between two or more parties to carry out the terms agreed upon. God established a blood covenant with Abraham. And during that time, a blood covenant relationship could only be broken by death. God told Abraham he would be the father of many nations, and Abraham believed Him. God wanted to establish a covenant with him that would allow Jesus to be born into the earth. It was through this covenant that they became *friends*. Abraham was called the friend of God because he believed and trusted the promises of God, and God counted him righteous (James 2:23).

Friendship is born out of commitments, vows, and promises kept between individuals. This covenant does not, however, give us the right to have the advantage in the relationship. Covenant relationship gives us the right to *give* the advantage. So if we have a true friend, what we should see in the relationship is a person who is more concerned with giving the advantage rather than taking the advantage. I have a friend, who is also a preacher, who got upset with me a while back because he wanted me to speak at his church more frequently. I had explained to him that I was focusing more on doing exactly what God told me to do rather than just doing a lot of speaking engagements simply because I was invited to preach. I remember his sharing with me that if I was really his covenant brother, I would preach at his church more often. I told him that if he was really *my* covenant brother, he would be more concerned with my seeking and obeying God than with what I could do for him. He said, "You're right. I repent!" True friends always seek to give each other the advantage and promote their well-being.

Many people establish friendships based on how the relationship can benefit them. These are the type of people we want to avoid. Have you ever known someone who was only concerned about how he or she could benefit from a relationship with you? It is usually the individual who is always calling on you for assistance (financial or emotional) but is never available when you are in need. This is not what friendship is all about. When we identify people in our lives who are takers, we need to reevaluate those relationships. Are you the only one giving all the time? I have been there, and it is not uncommon to feel spiritually and emotionally drained after dealing with their issues. These are the friends who always have convenient excuses as to why they can never reciprocate what you give.

FRIENDS HELP EQUIP US FOR OUR DESTINY

Proverbs 27:17 says, "Iron sharpeneth iron; so a man sharpeneth the countenance of his friend." Iron sharpens iron. This is the way it should be in our friendships. Friends sharpen one another for the greater things of God. We don't want to have friendships that dull our lives, but friendships that sharpen us and build us up through encouragement. Friends exchange strengths for weaknesses. Friends strengthen one another in areas they are strong in and are willing to receive help in areas where they are weak. A common goal in any good, solid relationship is to eliminate weaknesses. This empowers us to help one another fulfill the divine purposes and callings in our lives.

I have heard some foolishly say that they do not need relationships to be what God has called them to be. I find this hard to believe since our entire existence is based on relationships. Relationships are like bridges that are designed to take us from one level to another. Without the bridges, we would have gaps through which we would fall. God is a relationship God, and He has our destiny tied in with others. There are certain areas in our lives that we will simply not be able to reach without God-connected relationships.

Ecclesiastes 4:9–10 says, "Two are better than one; because they have a good reward for their labour. For if they fall, the one will lift up his fellow: but woe to him that is alone when he falleth; for he hath not another to help him up." We can accomplish much more with the help of others than we can alone. If you take a moment to examine your life, I'm sure you can see that you have accomplished many of your goals because of the relationships you have established.

THREE LEVELS OF FRIENDSHIP

When choosing friends, I always advise people to acknowledge the three levels, or chambers, of friendship. The three levels of friendship are modeled after the tabernacle in the Old Testament, which had an outer court, an inner court, and a holy of holies— the place behind the veil. The important thing to remember is that there should be very few people behind the veil in your life. Not everyone can or should be allowed access.

In the outer court are those we know by name. We treat them cordially as we come across them at work, church, and other limited social settings. They are acquaintances. Those in the inner court are those we visit or hang out with from time to time. We know some of their family, the names of their children, where they live, etc. We share things in common, and we enjoy their company. These are companions.

Then we have a select and limited few who are allowed behind the veil into our holy of holies. There should be only one or two people here—three at the most. These are the friends we've invited to hold our heart. Behind the veil, we've allowed them to see things that others will never see. There is intimacy behind the veil where we are vulnerable and exposed. Only the most trusted belong here. Holy of holies friends know our highest dreams, greatest achievements, and deepest secrets. They celebrate, encourage, admonish, and reprove whenever we need them and at any given time—lovingly, willingly, and unconditionally.

KEYS TO REMEMBER

When I think of friendship, one word comes straight to the forefront of my mind: *loyalty.* Loyalty is a big word. It cannot be demonstrated by simply saying "I am loyal." It is demonstrated by the decisions we make and the actions we take to be there for others. There are seven wisdom keys concerning friendship that I have found helpful in my life when evaluating relationships and keeping them in the proper perspective.

Key One: A Real Friend Will Comfort and Support You When You Are in Trouble

A true friend is there to comfort and support you when you are in need. When Job was in need, his friends showed up. "Now when Job's three friends heard of this evil that was come upon him, they came every one from his own place" (Job 2:11). When you were in a situation where you really needed someone to depend on, who showed up? Who was there? As a friend, it's important to be there in the times of need.

Key Two: A Friend Is Devoted

Job 6:14 in the Amplified Bible says, "To him who is about to faint and despair, kindness is due from his friend lest he forsake the fear of the Almighty." Well, we know the fear of the Lord is to respect God with the audacity to obey. When others we know are about to faint or fall into despair, kindness is due to those we call "friend." And when we show kindness to them, we also show honor and respect to God. In a sense, this is fascinating because my relationship with God is going to be based on my relationship with others. I can't say I love God whom I've never seen and hate my brother or sister I see every day.

If my friend is at the point where he or she may faint—cave in or quit—kindness is due to that friend from me. So out of respect to God, we willingly honor and respect our friends, realizing that the kindness shown is not only unto our friends but also unto God. Jesus said, "Inasmuch as ye have done this unto the least of these my brethren, ye have done it unto me" (Matthew 25:40).

Key Three: A Friend Loves Unconditionally

A true holy of holies friend loves you no matter what the situation is or what you've done. Once you've trusted this individual with access and information that most are not privy to, this relationship should have a certain level of trust and confidence. Do you feel comfortable sharing the most intimate and private details of your life with this person? Do you trust him or her enough to expose your secrets? At the end of the day, is there mutual, unconditional love and respect within the relationship?

Of course we must keep this in the proper perspective. If a person makes a mistake, as a friend you should be there for that person. However, if this person abuses this unconditional love by continuously or intentionally doing things that hurt or weaken the relationship, you may have to reevaluate the relationship.

Key Four: Friends Speak Constructively, Even When It Hurts

Friends speak the truth in love, even when it hurts. While it's good to appreciate the qualities in one another, true friends are there to give us constructive criticism when we need it. "Faithful are the wounds of a friend, but the kisses of an enemy are lavish and deceitful" (Proverbs 27:6 AMP). Faithful are the wounds of a true friend because they are said out of love in order to help us grow. However, by the same token, we have to be sure to discern a kiss. Not all kisses are from friends. Judas betrayed Jesus with a kiss. It was a kiss, but it was deceitful. Those who are full of flattery are not always true friends.

We also have to be careful not to relate wounds with enemies. Sometimes our friends will wound us. There are times when we don't want to hear or accept the truth because it hurts. But if you're my friend and you truly care about me, hurt me! So many people have walked away from relationships because they were wounded by someone they thought was an enemy. Someone told them they were being selfish, or they were walking in pride, or they should reevaluate some things; then they got offended and walked away from the relationship. But these are the kind of people we need in our lives—people who tell us the truth. I would rather my friends tell me the truth in love than allow me to go on in error, which may lead to my embarrassment or harm.

God blesses us with friends to help us learn, grow, and better ourselves. Aren't you tired of phonies? I am. Tell me the truth. It may hurt, but I'll get over it.

Key Five: A Friend Helps When You're Down

We talked about this some earlier. A friend will surely be there to pick you up when you're down. I'll never forget how my good friend Ken was there for me during one of the lowest points of my

life. We were in college at the time. I had hopes of playing football, but I was injured and couldn't play. My parents had just gone
through a divorce. I was hungry. And I was broke. Ken came by and
said, "Man, come on. We're going to go for a ride." We were college
students, we didn't have much; but what he had he was willing to
share. So we got into Ken's ol' faithful Lincoln, which we affection-
ately referred to as "the ark," and we went for a drive. That's what
friends do. There were many times that I wanted to give up, but
God put true friends in my life who wouldn't give up on me. When
you're up, everyone wants to be your friend. But who's there when
you're down? And who knows you well enough to know you're
down and is willing to stay there until you get back up?

Key Six: A Friend Has Intimate Knowledge of Your Affairs

In John 15:15 Jesus said, "Henceforth I call you not servants; for
the servant knoweth not what his lord doeth: but I have called you
friends; for all things that I have heard of my Father I have made
known unto you." Jesus said we are His friends because everything the Father has made known to Him, He has made known
to us. Servants don't have it like this. We are now in relationship
with God through and by the blood of Jesus. We now have fellowship and intimacy with our Father.

A friend has intimate knowledge of your affairs. The only people who need to know about your intimate affairs are the one or
two behind the veil—your holy of holies friends. Be very wise and
cautious about whom you equip with such private information.
You don't want to share private information with someone who
is jealous of what you have or who you are. You must have a dis-
cerning heart, even within the body of Christ. Some of us get so
caught up in the cross around the neck or the Christian T-shirt
that we feel at liberty to share personal details about our lives. Be
very careful how you handle your personal affairs.

Key Seven: A Friend Makes Your Life Better by Giving Good Advice

Proverbs 27:9 says, "Ointment and perfume rejoice the heart: so doth the sweetness of a man's friend by hearty counsel." Good friends give good advice. True friends care about our happiness and well-being. They will be quick to share good, godly counsel concerning situations and circumstances in our lives.

THE TRUEST, CLOSEST FRIENDS

Jesus is the perfect example of a true friend. We can relate all seven keys to Him. He comforts and supports. He is devoted. He loves us regardless of where we are or what we've done. He speaks constructively to us. He helps us when we're down. We can trust Him with our most intimate secrets and biggest dreams. His advice and counsel equip us to live life to the fullest. If you don't know Him, be sure to get to know this Friend who sticks closer than any brother. Even though we most likely will not be faced with a decision to die for our friends, His example teaches us that true friendship is marked by unconditional love and sacrifice. John 15:13 says, "No one has greater love [no one has shown stronger affection] than to lay down (give up) his own life for his friends" (AMP). Jesus said we are His friends if we obey His commandments to love the Lord our God with all our hearts, souls, minds, and strength. And we are to love our neighbors as we love ourselves. A true friend of Jesus will lay down his or her personal agenda and selfish desires in exchange for what pleases Him.

The word *friend* is more than just a title; it is a commitment. To be a true friend means we are willing to give at all times. To attract genuine friends in our lives, we must become one to others. When we do, we mirror God's relationship with us, which compels us to give the advantage. God loves us and wants us to make a commitment to love one another. True friends encourage one another in the things of God. They continue to support one another as they strive to live a life that is in line with the Word. Be prayerful when selecting friends. And be wise when choosing whom to share your life with, because the company you keep will ultimately determine the life you live.

CHOOSING A MATE

Your happiness is going to be based on whom you decide to share the rest of your life with.

About two years ago, I started a teaching series on relationships. One Sunday during the series, I asked all the single people in our congregation to stand. I was shocked to see that most of the congregation stood up! I thought to myself, *Why are so many of them still single? Why aren't more of these men and women making a connection?* These questions prompted me to teach on the subject of choosing a mate.

God has given single people the option to choose between the blessing and the curse where marriage is concerned. In other words, you can choose to have a blessed life or a cursed one. Deuteronomy 30:19 says, "I call heaven and earth to record this day against you, that I have set before you life and death, blessing and cursing: therefore choose life, that both thou and thy seed may live."

Choosing a mate is one of the most important decisions an individual will ever make in life. It's a decision that should not be made without first seeking wisdom from God, through His Word. Proverbs 4:11 in the Amplified Bible says, "I have taught you in the way of skillful and godly Wisdom [which is comprehensive insight into the ways and purposes of God]; I have led you in the paths of uprightness."

So what makes choosing a mate so important? Your happiness is going to be based on whom you decide to share the rest of your life with. Choose well, because it can either be days of heaven on earth, or hell on earth.

According to a report by the Barna Group, one out of every five adults has never been married. Of those who have married, one out of three has been divorced at least once. In addition, the report revealed that the divorce rate among born-again Christians is identical to that of non-Christians![1]

Christian singles must make wise decisions in order to avoid becoming one of the aforementioned statistics.

CHOOSING A MATE GOD'S WAY VERSUS THE WORLD'S WAY

Myriad TV shows and advertisements target singles with the subliminal message that *it is okay to do whatever you want with whomever you want to do it.* I want to encourage all singles to change their thinking and begin to believe God has a plan that is greater than any plan the world or society has to offer (Jeremiah 29:11; Ephesians 3:20).

Marriage was created by God and is part of His plan for those who desire to enter this covenant relationship. Unfortunately, many people remain single because they make unwise choices when it comes to choosing a mate.

The following are two major points I would like for singles to keep in mind:

Do Not Seek a Mate—Seek God

Please do not misunderstand what I am saying here. Of course there is practical action you must take when you are interested in someone. However, you should have your priorities in order. Do not make seeking a mate a higher priority than seeking a relationship with God. Your relationship with Him should be your first priority.

I met my wife, Taffi, while I was attending college. I'll never forget the day I first saw Taffi. She was walking down a pathway on campus, wearing a cute flowery sundress. Her skin was a beautiful golden brown. She *really* caught my attention! But I thought maybe she was too good for me.

One day, while I was relaxing between classes in one of the student lounges, Taffi walked in and said, "I'm interested in you" and walked out. Flattered by her words, I thought, *She's going to pursue me! That's great!* But it didn't turn out that way. From that point on, she acted as if I didn't exist. I later found out she was thinking, *If you're too stupid to know what to do with that information, you don't deserve me anyway.*

I wanted a wife, so I began to pray about it. I wanted God to get involved. I asked the Lord for a wife, and I was very specific—even down to big, pretty legs! I submitted my request, and in the meantime I got busy pursuing the things of God. We had a group meeting on campus called Search and Research. Basically we would get together for two or more hours and search the Scriptures and study the Word of God. You could set your clock by Taffi when it came to showing up at these meetings. I could see she was as hungry for the Word of God as I was.

During one of our Bible studies, I noticed Taffi was sitting across from me. As always, we opened our Bible study with prayer. While we were praying, God told me to open my eyes. Taffi was wearing a pair of capri pants, and when I opened my eyes and saw those big, pretty legs, I quickly closed my eyes—*tightly!*—and started praying in the Spirit. Again, the Lord said, "Open your eyes. I'm trying to show you she's the one you've been praying for."

The revelation did not come to me because I came to Bible study looking to be hooked up with somebody. The connection between Taffi and me was made because we were focused on hooking up with God. When you are busy hooking up with Him, He gets involved and gives you the hookup!

There are many Christian singles who desire to be married. I say to you: seek God and find out what He wants you to do for the kingdom. Pursue the things of God. Find out what it is He wants you to do for the kingdom and get busy doing it.

Respect Your Parents' Judgment

I will preface this point by first saying: if your parents do not make wise decisions, or if their thinking and speaking does not line up with the Word of God, then you may need to seek the advice of a mature Christian advisor or mentor. However, as a whole, most parents know you better than anyone else, and they want the best for you. Therefore, they would most likely demonstrate good judgment in helping you choose a spouse. Often parents will ask questions you may not think of asking.

BE INFORMED

During the dating process is the time to find out all the information you need to make an informed decision. Here are some important questions to ask and get answers to while you are dating.

Is This Person a Christian?

Do not be unequally yoked together with unbelievers (2 Corinthians 6:14). I would not advise you to marry someone whose beliefs or moral values go against what you believe as a Christian. You could be setting yourself up for a lot of strange things, and a yoke of bondage. Choose a Christian mate in order to facilitate true harmony in your relationship (2 Corinthians 6:15 AMP).

A woman once said to me, "Pastor, the Lord told me to marry my boyfriend. So I am getting ready to get married." I said, "Praise the Lord." The first question I asked her was, "Is he a Christian?" She said, "Well...." I knew right then something was wrong. He was not a Christian, and yet she was saying the Lord told her to marry him. I asked, "Why would God say to do one thing in His written Word and then tell you to do something else in a spoken word?" I basically told her that she had missed God because apparently her thinking was not lining up with His Word. As I continued to talk to her, I found that she was more concerned about having sex than seeking God's will; therefore she was willing to compromise her values as a Christian.

Please understand, it is not wise to compromise your values to keep someone. Do not be so desperate that you cannot make a wise decision. Always be willing to walk away if you are put in a position where you have to compromise your Christian beliefs.

What Kind of Christian Is Your Choice?

These days it is not enough to simply ask if someone is a Christian. The Bible says a tree is known by the fruit that it bears. What kind of fruit does this person produce? We as Christians should bear the fruit of the Spirit (Galatians 5:22–23).

Does the Person Have a Commitment to Love and Obey God?

What is this person's personal history? How does this person acknowledge the Word in his or her personal life? Is he or she a committed Christian?

Are the Two of You Spiritually Compatible?

The Word is spiritual. Therefore, you cannot get an understanding of your spiritual compatibility without first having a good amount of fellowship and communication regarding the Word. Are you compatible where prayer is concerned? Do you both like to pray? Do you pray together? Do you both agree it is important to read the Bible daily and get an understanding of God's Word? Do you both agree that it is important to meditate on the Word? Do you both agree that it is important to live by the Word?

Do You Agree on the Major Doctrines of the Bible?

It is important to know what the major doctrines of the Bible are so that you can discover if you share the same beliefs. Take time to discuss the doctrines of baptism, the Trinity, righteousness, and faith. These are great topics to discuss on your dates. Resist the urge to get romantic too soon while dating. Instead, engage in lengthy conversations regarding very important issues that will have a positive or negative effect on your relationship. Remember, the brother or sister needs to pass your checklist first!

Do You Agree on What Church You Will Attend?

If you have different beliefs or attend different churches, you will definitely need to discuss where you will attend church. This discussion should take place before the marriage, especially if you are planning to have children.

Do You Agree on How You Will Spend Your Time and Money?

This topic definitely needs to be discussed, especially if both of you have careers. Ask questions like: How do you spend your personal quality time? Do you spend all your time in front of the television? Are you spending your time shopping? Are you spending all of your time hanging out with the guys? You would also like to know how much time your potential spouse is willing to commit to spending with you. You have to have an understanding *before* the marriage that spending time together—making it a priority—is essential. Keep the romance throughout the marriage. You have to be willing to maintain throughout the marriage whatever it took to get your mate from the start.

You should have the same financial goals. How important are saving and investing? Does this person spend money wisely or foolishly? Is this person a tither and a giver?

Can You Trust This Person?

Have you spent enough quality time with this person to intelligently answer this question? Trust is built over time. Be sure to really get to know each other and establish mutual respect and confidence.

Has This Person Given You Any Reason Not to Trust What He or She Has Said or Done?

Has this person said or done something that later did not agree with what he or she had said previously? For example, he or she says, "I'm not dating anyone other than you." Then, when the two of you are in a restaurant, you bump into someone who says to your date, "I sure enjoyed last night." That is a reason to check out right then and there! If someone has given a reason not to be trusted while you are dating, most likely there will be reasons for lack of trust when you're married.

How Does He or She Handle Adversity?

Have you ever seen this person deal with adversity? Your date looks real cool, calm, and collected when you are out, but have you seen his or her behavior when the business deal did not work out favorably? How does this person respond when life doesn't go as planned? What happens when hardship comes? Does this person get depressed or become suicidal? Does he or she get angry, fly off the handle, and lose control? Prior to committing your life to someone, you should have already observed how he or she operates in the midst of adversity.

Does This Person Trust God or Fall into Unbelief Regularly?

When adversity does show up, do you see him or her standing on the Word with a positive attitude, quoting the Word, believing God, and remaining motivated? Or do you see this individual depressed, speaking negatively, murmuring, and complaining? Notice what is going on in the midst of a situation. You should want a mate whose trust and confidence are in God and His Word, regardless of the circumstances.

Has This Person Ever Displayed Anger?

You do not need to walk down the aisle with anyone you have not seen angry. Don't think for a moment your love interest does not get angry. Think about it. Haven't you been angry before? We all get angry. Do you know the two people in the Bible who got angry the most? God and Jesus! The anger of the Lord was kindled many times. Jesus was in the temple and got angry at the money changers. He turned over tables and started whipping people. Be realistic about it. If God and Jesus got angry, do you think you will marry a man or woman who does not ever get angry? You need to know how this person expresses anger.

Have You Seen This Individual Angry with You?

What is this person like when angry with you? If your future husband or wife gets angry, loses control, and mentally or physically abuses you, that should be a big red flag.

Does This Person Resolve Conflict in a Biblical Way?

This is part of the previous question. When there was a conflict between the two of you, how was it handled? Was it handled in a biblical manner, by seeking wisdom from the Word? Were you in agreement on how it was handled? Was it resolved peacefully, or did the two of you simply ignore or fail to deal with it? The manner in which you handle conflict now is an indication as to how you will handle it in your marriage.

Does This Person Ask for Forgiveness?

I think it is terrible when couples have disagreements and one or both of them never ask for forgiveness or deal with the issues at all. Instead, they just choose to pick up and move on as if the incident never took place. How can a conflict be resolved when it is ignored? Consider whether this person acknowledges when he or she is wrong. Also, is he or she willing to forgive?

Ladies, Does He Have a Way to Provide for You?

The first time I asked my wife to marry me, she said no. I said, "I can't believe you said no." Taffi said, "Baby, we came to the park in your mama's station wagon. You are living with your mama and working part time. You can't take care of us yet, but when you get a good job and stability, my answer will definitely be yes."

At first it was a hard pill for me to swallow, but I eventually understood where she was coming from. As a man, it is my responsibility to support my wife and household. Ladies, let a man be a man by allowing him to own up to his responsibilities. If he cannot financially support a household, he is not ready to be a husband. Love and support him enough to give him time to be a good provider and a stable head of the household.

Is He or She Responsible with Money?

Are you about to marry a shopaholic? Is your potential spouse an emotional spender? In other words, whenever upset, does this person go out and spend money on clothes, shoes, or other things? Does he or she spend large amounts of money on things and try to keep it from you? How your future spouse treats money now is a clear indication of how your husband or wife will spend money after you are married.

Is Your Future Spouse a Good Example for Children?

One day you are probably going to have children with this person. Is he or she the example you want your children to follow?

What Issues Do You Agree or Disagree On?

Be sure to make this one of the topics of conversation while you are dating. Get the issues resolved during the dating stage. You do not want these issues to creep up and cause problems after you are married.

Is There Self-Control over His or Her Sex Drive?

If the person you are considering marrying does not have control over his or her sex drive while you are dating, chances are there will be no control once you are married, which could possibly lead to extramarital affairs.

Does Your Prospective Mate Respect You?

Are your opinions respected? Men, are you dating someone who wants to make all the decisions and doesn't respect your opinions at all? Is this person controlling and very needy, and unwilling to listen to anything you have to say? Ladies, do you have a man who will not even open the door for you, but he will open the door for others? Are you dating a man who will not pay attention to your opinions or feelings?

If your potential mate doesn't respect you before you are married, he or she most likely won't respect you after you are married.

Are You Consulted in Decision Making?

Do not marry someone who will not consult you before making important decisions. If you do, once you are married, your mate will feel entitled to make major decisions such as purchasing a car, taking a trip, or making plans without first discussing them with you.

Is There a Mutual Submission Between the Two of You?

The Bible says in Ephesians 5:21 to submit ourselves—one to the other—in the fear of the Lord. That means a husband must submit himself to his wife, by obeying what God tells him to do as a husband, and a wife must submit herself to her husband, by obeying what God tells her. Marriage is about mutual submission.

Is He or She Truly Open to Your Input?

Are you in a relationship with someone who really does not want to hear what you have to say? You do not want to spend your life with a partner who makes you feel dumb or treats you as if you have nothing to contribute.

How Does Your Prospective Mate Treat Other People?

Have you seen this person interact with others? How does he or she act around other people? It is easy to pretend when the two of you are out alone, but you must observe your date's treatment of others. How does he or she act in a group setting or with family and friends? How does he or she treat your family and friends?

Do You Know What He or She Struggles with in His or Her Personal Life?

You must date long enough to find out what this person struggles with, even if you have to ask. Don't be afraid to put it out there. This is so important because you do not want to end up in a marriage with someone who is struggling with something that you were not aware of. For instance, suppose he or she has issues with pornography, homosexuality, or drug addiction. These are things you need to know long before you say "I do."

Can You Live with Your Prospective Mate's Current Faults?

He or she may not handle money very well. Can you live with that? Or perhaps the individual has been deceitful. Can you live with that? Maybe your potential spouse has an eating disorder. Can you live with that problem? Whatever the issue is, you need to have open and honest communication about it before getting married.

Is This Person Giving?

If the person you want to marry is interested only in receiving, and rarely (if ever) in giving, that will be a problem. This behavior indicates selfishness. In a marriage, you need someone to encourage you, lift you up, and give to you unselfishly. You want someone who looks for ways to give to you and bless you.

Do the Two of You Communicate Effectively?

Open communication is essential to a successful marriage. As a couple, do you effectively communicate your feelings and ideas?

Do you know how to tell each other what you need in the relationship and how you feel about the relationship?

Is Your Prospective Mate Your Best Friend?

Friendship is the foundation of a good marriage. Friends will lay down their lives for friends. Have you chosen someone who will lay down his or her life for you? In other words, does your potential mate sacrifice self-interests or plans for you? If you marry someone who is not willing to make these sacrifices, you may end up with someone who is undependable and inaccessible.

If You or Your Potential Mate Is Divorced, Do You Both Know Why the Divorce Took Place?

To begin the healing process after a divorce, ask God to forgive you for your part in the divorce and ask your former spouse for forgiveness as well. This allows healing to take place and a fresh start to begin. Then, ask yourself, *Am I looking for someone to come and rescue me and take care of me, or am I looking for someone I can give to? Have I really changed—spiritually, emotionally, and morally?* These are also important questions you should answer before you accept a marriage proposal. This will assist you in making a wise choice the second time around.

As a pastor and a former therapist, one of the things that has really amazed me through the years is that different people come with the same problems, but they have different perspectives about their problems because their perspectives are based on a different set of criteria. And they're all making decisions based on that set criteria.

As Christians, we must establish the Word of God as the basis for every decision we make in our lives. When we understand and live this reality, we end up in a good place because we're making wise decisions.

ESTABLISHING MARITAL BLISS

The Word of God teaches us everything we need to
know about the opposite sex.

꩜ Many couples begin their marriages eager to live the fairy
tale they've read about, watched on the big screen, or listened to
while dancing to their favorite love songs. Movies, books, and
songs can paint a picture of marital bliss that has very little to do
with reality. For instance, one of the most popular fairy tales of
all time concerning love and happiness is the story of Cinderella.
After being mistreated for years at the hands of her stepmother,
this young woman finds love with the most eligible bachelor in
town—the prince! He rescues her from her dismal existence, and
they live happily ever after.

However, in reality, when a couple says "I do" and attempts
to live out their fairy tale of a happily-ever-after marriage, it isn't
long before reality sets in, and they realize life is not a fairy tale.
It takes a tremendous amount of work and effort, by both parties,
to achieve marital bliss. I often tell people, the word *work* is not a
dirty word. When a couple is building a successful marriage, the
willingness to work at it will create a beautiful masterpiece that
portrays two lives joined together as one.

I believe one of the causes of the high divorce rate today is the
microwave mentality that has developed through the years. Many
people want something of value without putting in time and

effort. It's the small foxes that destroy the vine. In other words, sometimes it's the small things that are blown out of proportion that ultimately cause relationships to end. Some of the most minor incidents can grow into a whirlwind of strife and bitterness if left unresolved.

Most of the strife that enters a marriage stems from personality conflicts. Although two are now one, there are still different opinions, personalities, and viewpoints. Therefore, there will be times when arguments will arise. However, it is not the arguments that destroy marriages, but how the conflicts are handled.

In the midst of counseling sessions, I have discovered that many married couples have never received instruction in conflict resolution. When a couple has not learned the proper conflict resolution strategies, they resort to settling their differences by fighting.

FOUR IMPROPER FIGHTING STYLES

Here are four fighting styles to avoid when dealing with conflicts or problems.

The Eskimo Style

In this case, one or both spouses freeze up after an argument and ignore the situation altogether, hoping time will take care of it. They withdraw emotionally and nurse their wounds. This is more commonly known as the silent treatment. As a result, one or both parties become bitter because a mutual resolution is not reached.

The Cowboy Style

This is the "shoot 'em up an' leave 'em for dead!" style. In the heat of passion, couples tend to say things they do not mean. Harsh words can hurt, causing a lot of damage to a marriage and severely limiting any chances of reconciling differences.

The Houdini Style

When conflicts arise, one or both parties become escape artists. He or she does not like conflict and will avoid it as much as possible. Rather than face an issue head-on, this individual will just leave. Often this spouse will turn to destructive behaviors such as drinking, excessive shopping, sitting in front of the television for hours, or overeating. He or she will do whatever it takes to avoid dealing with the situation.

The World Boxing Association Style

Here we have one or both parties handling conflicts with their fists. He or she may begin to deal with an issue rationally, but anger often takes over, and the individual becomes physically abusive. This spouse may be an abuser who is in need of counseling.

No matter what situation you may face as a couple, realize that fighting is not the best way to resolve conflict. Pray about it and seek God's wisdom in every circumstance.

PRAYER IS ALWAYS THE SOLUTION

When facing conflict in marriage, we need answers right away. The first step toward resolution is prayer—heartfelt, Word-based prayer. It is important to step away from the situation long enough to hear from God. If you feel you need to take a walk to get away, by all means do so. Often couples are too angry to call a temporary truce in order to seek God, but it is the best thing to do.

Couples should ask the Father to reveal to them their roles in causing the conflict. God wants us to judge ourselves. When we do, He will help us bring balance and perspective to any situation. It takes a mature person to accept his or her responsibility for a problem. I know it is human nature to respond in negative ways when accused. However, when we reevaluate the situation and pray before allowing our emotions to get the best of us, we are able to accurately judge ourselves so that we can understand how we contributed to the problem.

As you seek God, ask Him if you're the problem: "Am I being unreasonable? Am I being selfish?" I do that all the time! "God, where do I take responsibility here? Show me, and I will commit to change."

BEGINNING THE HEALING PROCESS

To begin the healing process, I often advise couples to plan a formal peace conference in a quiet setting where both parties can face the issue head-on. But timing is of the essence. It is not wise to try to tackle an issue while tired or stressed-out, or when the children are awake. Trying to discuss issues during family time is counterproductive. Taffi and I often wait until after spending time with our children. Then we may go out for a quiet dinner or for a long walk and discuss the problem without any distractions. Couples must purposely schedule quiet time for peace talks.

There will come a time in our relationships when we will discover that our emotions are not stable enough to properly deal with a conflict the moment it happens. During these times, it is wise to put certain problems on the shelf until the time is right to deal with them. Waiting until our emotions are under control helps us to resolve the conflict in an amicable manner.

In addition to prayer and peace talks, here are some principles to remember when handling conflicts.

Maintain a Positive Outlook

Dissolve all fear by reinforcing the positive. Begin by saying, "I love you with all of my heart, and I am committed to our marriage."

Be Willing to Take the Blame

Bring to the discussion whatever it is that you received from God in prayer. Acknowledge and take responsibility for your role in the conflict or problem. You can say something like, "Honey, the Lord told me to judge myself. I discovered I have a tendency to blame you for things because I want to protect my own feelings, and I don't want to take responsibility." Your spouse probably already knows what you have done, so go ahead and confess it.

Apologize

Never underestimate the power of an apology. A sincere apology produces great results. It heals, soothes, restores, and brings joy back into a relationship. Only prideful people find it difficult to apologize.

Express Your Hurt Instead of Hostility

Hurt is a legitimate response to disappointment or offense. Often men hide the fact that they are hurt. However, when those hurt feelings are not properly dealt with, they remain locked inside until they mature into anger, resentment, or bitterness. Whenever you feel angry, ask yourself, *Why am I angry?* People do not feel angry without a reason. The anger can sometimes be traced back to an offense that caused hurt.

Deal with hurt feelings as they arise. There is nothing weak about admitting to your spouse that something he or she said hurt you! You will be surprised what it will do for your relationship.

Once that hurt is dealt with, you will no longer have to bear the weight of it on your heart and mind. Ephesians 4:26 cautions us to avoid going to bed without resolving the issues that caused anger. Even if you have to say, "We'll talk about it tomorrow, but for now, please forgive me," that is better than sleeping on the couch or passing messages to your spouse through your children.

Make Direct Statements

One definition of integrity is *straightforwardness*. Hints and offhand remarks accomplish very little. Say what you mean. For example, "You hurt me when you decided to spend all night watching television." Don't hint and say, "Well, maybe I was a little disappointed when you spent last night watching TV, but it's really no big deal." Be honest about your feelings.

Avoid Absolute Statements Using "Always" and "Never"

Peace talks are quickly sabotaged when accusatory statements are made, such as, "You always do this!" or "You never help me around the house!" Using the words *you*, *always*, and *never* will immediately place the accused person on the defensive. Instead, tell your spouse how you feel. "I feel left out of your life because you are so busy with work." "I feel frustrated about our money situation." "I feel overwhelmed with all the housework left undone." A softer approach to making your point opens the door for further communication. Remember, effective communication builds successful marriages.

Be Solution-Centered

Both spouses should always come together focused on the solution rather than the problem. Resist the urge to focus only on the problem. For every problem, there is a solution. Be open and willing to discover the solution to your problem. It is the perfect opportunity to be a team player and put problem-solving skills to work.

Seek Godly Counsel

Church leaders are not the only ones who can offer you sound advice and godly counsel. Mature believers can also offer couples wisdom and guidance. Although secular counseling is available, it is not always a good idea to seek advice from people who cannot give biblical advice. Choose a Christian mediator, and remain faithful and consistent throughout the healing process until you see results.

A crucial point to remember is to seek counsel for yourself, not your mate. When someone comes to see me for counseling and points the finger at his or her spouse, I shift the focus back to the accuser. Why? Because it takes two to tango! Problems in a marriage do not surface because of one person. Sometimes it takes a professional mediator to help bring down the walls that exist between the two people.

As couples, we must be willing to apply practical, biblical principles in our marriages. If not, we will continue to be susceptible to the schemes of the enemy. We cannot expect lasting, positive results in our marriages until we begin to train ourselves to seek God first, by researching His Word for answers to our problems. We can then apply that knowledge to our relationships, which will bring about significant change in our lives.

WINNING IN THE BATTLE OF THE SEXES

Men and women have different needs. That should be no surprise to anyone. However, discovering what those needs are can sometimes be challenging. The good news is it's not as difficult as it seems. While it appears that men and women are from two different planets, God has outlined in His Word ways we can be sure to meet each other's needs. But both people must be willing to understand their spouse and make the necessary adjustments.

When we search the Scriptures, we discover that the Word of God teaches us everything we need to know about the opposite sex. For example, Genesis 3:17 says because of Adam's failure to obey God's Word, the ground would be cursed and his labor would be hard. As a result, we see a man's greatest need is for significance and achievement. Men are naturally task-oriented, and they measure success by what they achieve in life, often as it relates to their jobs or careers.

Women are naturally more relational. Eve was created for and in the midst of a relationship. Therefore, a woman's primary concern in life is to nurture her loved ones, which usually occurs as she manages her home, raises her children, and strengthens her family.

When it comes to relationships, most men are terrified of not being able to do their part, which has a direct impact on their self-worth. Many women do not understand this fear and often react indifferently. Men skillfully hide these feelings until they can no longer contain them. However, if couples would gain a clear understanding of the fears men face, they could work together more peacefully to build healthier, more satisfying marital relationships.

Ladies, here are some basic principles that, when consistently applied, will show your husband that you love him and support his efforts to be the best he can be.

Show Him Respect

Men thrive when they are respected. It amplifies their self-esteem. However, when a man is disrespected, it goes right to the core of his being and deeply wounds him, zapping his energy and motivation. I am not referring to a husband who is lazy, selfish, and self-centered. I'm referring to a man who is doing his best to provide for and protect his wife and family.

Be Your Husband's Best Friend

If a man is feeling pressure, it may be difficult for him to express how he feels. When he does open up, he needs his wife to be a loving and receptive listener, showing interest and concern. Help him to see that God has always brought the two of you through hard times, and He won't stop now. Remind him that he is God's son and God lives in him. Communicate to him that wisdom is the principle thing in his life. Then pray together to receive the wisdom you need for the situation.

Tell Him He Is Significant

A man needs to know that he matters and is important to his family. If he thinks he is worthless, his motivation is depleted. He will feel insecure, inferior, and inadequate. You can prevent him from feeling this way by telling him how much you love him and need him in your life. Also remind him through words and actions of his importance to his children and other family members.

Praise Him Publicly

Never criticize your husband in front of others or allow anyone else to do it. A great deal of damage is done to a man when you put him down or disrespect him in front of other people. Instead, stand up for your man and let him see you doing it. Brag about the wonderful things he has done for you and what he means to you.

Light His Fire!

It is no secret that physical love is a primary need for men. But that does not mean he always wants to be the initiator. In fact, most husbands want their wives to be initiators also. A spontaneous woman is a real turn-on for most men! Husbands need to know that their wives desire sexual intimacy with them. A wife should make her husband feel he is the best thing that ever came into her life! In addition, do not be afraid to admire your husband and share that admiration with him. I love it when Taffi says, "Oooh! Look at my fine husband!" I usually just smile and say jokingly, "Aaaw, hush, girl." But the truth is I hang on her every word. And then I walk with my chest a little broader and my head a little higher. Ladies, do that for your man, even if he acts as though it's no big deal. In reality, it goes a long way!

WHAT A WOMAN NEEDS

Genesis 3:16 sheds light on why women think and act the way they do: "Unto the woman he said, I will greatly multiply thy sorrow and thy conception; in sorrow thou shalt bring forth children; and thy desire shall be to thy husband, and he shall rule over thee."

A woman has two primary concerns: family and security. Remember, Eve was created from the rib of Adam. Her needs are met through close, meaningful relationships. Family is important to a woman. Her "desire" for her husband stems from her longing for an intimate friendship and relationship with him. The "sorrow" in rearing her children means that their safety, education, and well-being are a great concern for her.

It is easy to see why security is so important to a woman. Although she may marry a man who gets paid on commission, she would feel more comfortable if he had a steady paycheck.

Likewise, she may settle for a one-bedroom apartment, but she would probably rather live in a home large enough for her family.

Men, if we do not understand our wives, it will be easy to dishonor their roles and concerns. Furthermore, men who demean the roles of women as nurturers, by criticizing their concerns or ignoring them altogether, will drive a wedge between them and their wives, ultimately destroying their marriages.

God has given us, as men, special instructions on how to treat our wives. He knows that as men we prefer to hear "just the facts." That is why He directs us clearly in Scripture: "Husbands, love your wives, even as Christ also loved the church, and gave himself for it" (Ephesians 5:25). The crucial element that we need to focus on in this Scripture is the two words "even as." In what ways does God show His love to us?

Husbands, as we consider the unconditional love God shows to the church, we can gain insight into the kind of love for our wives God expects us to provide.

Spend Time with Her

Hasn't God always been there when you needed to talk to Him? When your wife wants to talk, she wants and needs you to listen. Do not ignore her because there is a game on TV or a good article in the newspaper. Remember, her basic needs are for closeness and security. Your wife wants to feel that you are her best friend. She wants to hear your perspective on the issues she faces.

Although it may not seem like a big deal to you, being able to discuss and share even the little things fosters a sense of intimacy and trust for her. Remember she is your first priority. I have seen some men use the ministry as an excuse for not having time for their wives. If you put the ministry or your job before your wife, you are out of the order that God has set for the family. One-on-one, attentive communication is necessary to fulfill her need for intimacy.

Be Her Soul Mate

Endeavor to be so close to your wife that the two of you are thinking the same thoughts. It is possible to be so unified in your spirit that when you open your mouth to say something, she is able to finish the sentence.

Be Romantic

To a woman, romance does not begin with sex! A woman desires nonsexual touching; this makes her feel special. Foreplay does not begin in the bedroom. It begins early in the morning and lasts all day. Demonstrate your unconditional love for her through your words, affection, and actions throughout the day. Then sex will be more enjoyable for both of you.

Do Your Share of Housework

The day you got married, you formed a partnership with your wife that affects every area of your life—even housework! Whatever she asks you to do around the house, do it. And don't pout or sulk while doing it. Take the initiative to help out before she asks.

Today women are busier than ever before, and most have full-time jobs outside of the home. Your wife does not want to return home in the evening to work another eight hours cooking, doing laundry, taking care of the children, and paying bills. If you want more affection from her, help her! A husband should be his wife's partner in every sense of the word.

Understand Your Wife

My marriage was revolutionized after I began to understand Taffi's needs as a woman. There are two scriptural reasons why you must understand your wife's needs. First, you cannot love your wife as God requires you to unless you understand her. Second, you cannot submit "one to another in the fear of God" unless those needs are met (Ephesians 5:21). Fear and insecurity rise within her when her needs for security, intimacy, and love are threatened or unmet. If your wife is fearful or reserved, evaluate the relationship. Ask yourself these questions:

- *Which one of my wife's needs is not being met?*

- *Am I being transparent enough with her? Do I tell her everything she needs to know?*

- *Am I telling her how I feel and what I am thinking?*

- *Do I cherish her?*

- *Does she feel financially secure?*

- *Am I taking care of our home?*

- *Have I allowed other things to take priority over her?*

I am a strong believer in balance. The Bible says a false balance is an abomination to God (Proverbs 11:1). While we must live according to the Word and apply the spiritual principles found in it, there are some practical principles we have to do in the natural to gain and maintain a healthy marriage. Many times believers go too far to the left or right. Balance is essential. When we use wisdom, and apply the spiritual along with the natural, we build a strong foundation for our marriages. In addition, we must make sure we are not an enemy to our marriages, consumed by the "inner-me."

When we achieve the balance God wants us to have, our marriages will look more and more like the fairy tales we first dreamed they would be!

RAISING SUCCESSFUL CHILDREN

When we follow the Word of God as it relates to raising our children, we see positive results.

⁑ Our children are gifts from God. There are times when we are made to wonder if this is true, but children are truly a blessing. I can attest to the fact that there are days when parenting feels more like a curse than a blessing. Those are the times when I take a moment to remember what the Bible says about children. Psalm 127:3 says, "Lo, children are an heritage of the LORD: and the fruit of the womb is his reward." This Scripture has a two-fold meaning. First, it explains the value of children, and then it speaks of the blessing they are to us.

Children are our heritage. One definition of the Hebrew word for *heritage* is "assignment." In the original Hebrew translation, Psalm 127:3 actually says, "Lo, children are an assignment of the Lord."

While our children are living in our homes, we have the opportunity to impart biblical principles that will enable them to fulfill God's purpose for their lives. As parents, we are responsible for training them in the ways of righteousness. They are our assignments, which God has entrusted to us.

It is important that we see our children the same way God sees them. Isaiah 8:18 says, "I and the children whom the LORD hath given me are for signs and for wonders in Israel from the LORD of hosts." Our sons and daughters are vessels God desires to use for

His glory. So, despite the hassle we go through just to get children to do their homework or brush their teeth, we cannot forget that God desires to use them as signs and wonders in these last days.

We are to recognize the gifts and callings God has placed within each child. When we help our sons and daughters to understand the Word of God, they will begin to develop a God-consciousness, which will increase their level of faith. As a result, they will begin to demonstrate to others what it means to be joined with and blessed of the Father!

Our children do not have to wait until they are adults to be used by God. Samson, Samuel, and Jesus were only boys when they began demonstrating the power of God in their lives. Size and age are irrelevant. Therefore, encourage your children to see themselves laying hands on the sick and seeing them recover. We can also help them create an inner image of themselves being used by God to prophesy, teach, intercede, and operate under His anointing. Further, it is important that they know we honor the call of God on their lives.

TRAINING THEM GOD'S WAY

God is a parent, and He knows children need discipline. Some need it more than others, but every child has to be disciplined from time to time. Proverbs 13:24 says, "He who spares his rod hates his son, but he who loves him disciplines him promptly" (NKJV). In recent years, there have been numerous books, articles, TV shows, and other media sources in which various people have taken a stand against the biblical principle of spanking. This demonstrates how society is being influenced by the world's way of doing things versus God's way. The world's way of thinking leads to unruly, undisciplined children who think they can do whatever they choose without any consequences. Children are not mature enough to always make wise decisions. The Bible says,

"Foolishness is bound up in the heart of a child, but the rod of discipline will drive it far from him" (Proverbs 22:15 AMP).

Sparing the rod has nothing to do with child abuse! Correction is a sign of love. However, bruises are a sign of abuse, not discipline. A spanking should never leave marks on a child's body, but on his or her conscience. All discipline, including spanking, should be done in love, not anger. Exhibiting harshness and cruelty is bad parenting. Cruel parents produce poorly behaved children. While I believe in spanking, I do not believe in misappropriating discipline in any way. The Bible also commands parents not to provoke their children to anger (Ephesians 6:4). God gave children to parents to guide them and teach them God's way of doing things. The Word of God admonishes us to "bring them up in the nurture and admonition of the Lord" (Ephesians 6:4).

When we follow the Word of God as it relates to raising our children, we see positive results. The Word is true and it works! On the other hand, we have seen how the world's way continues to fail.

There is no doubt about it, parenting according to biblical principles has proven to be the most effective system (2 Samuel 22:31). Taffi and I have consistently used the Word of God as our guide to parenting, and we can see positive results not only in our children but also in ourselves as parents.

Proverbs 22:6 says, "Train up a child in the way he should go: and when he is old, he will not depart from it." To *train* means "to mold character; to instruct by exercise" and "to drill."[1] There is a huge difference between teaching and training. For example, we can teach our sons and daughters the importance of personal hygiene by explaining the necessity of brushing their teeth. But to train them to value the practice of personal hygiene, we must get them up every morning and go through the personal hygiene procedures with them. Training reinforces what is taught, and in the process we are molding our children's character through exercise and regimentation.

GOOD OLD-FASHIONED HOME TRAINING

In our society, we do not have to go far to see that there are many children in need of some good old-fashioned home training! Some of them blatantly disrespect adults by answering them with terms like, *huh, what, yeah,* and so on. And if that isn't bad enough, some children are so disrespectful they even use profanity when speaking to adults, including their own parents. I'm glad my mother and father didn't go for that! Neither did Taffi's parents. My wife and I are strong believers in discipline and respect. For example, we tell our children it is important to show respect to adults, elders, and others who have authority over them by saying, "Yes, ma'am," "No, ma'am," "Yes, sir," and "No, sir." It is also important to have good manners and show the proper respect by saying "please," "excuse me," and "thank you."

In addition, we must train our children to control themselves, because nothing can be imparted into children who are undisciplined. A child who is out of control in public is out of control at home. Many parents blame school officials when they are called and informed that their children are misbehaving. We should not get angry with school administrators if we know that our children do not have proper home training. It only makes matters worse. As parents, whenever someone is having a problem with our children, we need to point the finger at ourselves. It is our responsibility to be sure our children are well behaved.

Failure to train our children the way the Bible teaches can go a lot deeper than receiving a phone call from a teacher or principal. When we fail to discipline and train our children, we invite a curse or an empowerment to fail upon our families. This is evident in the story of Eli. First Samuel 3:13–14 says, "For I have told him that I will judge his house for ever for the iniquity which he knoweth; because his sons made themselves vile, and he restrained them not. And therefore I have sworn unto the house of Eli, that the iniquity of Eli's house shall not be purged with sacrifice nor offering for ever."

Eli allowed his sons to sin before God by sleeping with prostitutes in God's house and eating the sacrificial portions that were holy. Eli's passive parenting angered God. As a result, he and his sons lost their positions as priests in the temple and died. When we turn a blind eye to our children's misbehavior, we open the door for the negative consequences that are sure to follow.

Here are three types of parenting styles we need to be aware of. The first two occur when we do not trust God or follow His methods of training children. We should all strive to execute the third parenting style, as it guarantees the positive results we desire to have for our children.

Isolation

Some parents are fearful because of the many negative influences and perilous activities that occur in our society, and as a result, they tend to isolate their children in an attempt to protect them. Many times these children are not even allowed to play with other children in the neighborhood. Aside from the contact they have with people at school and church, they are not allowed to form relationships outside of the home. These children can grow up lacking the necessary social skills needed for them to interact with others in a positive and productive manner.

Passivity

Often, passive parents feel defeated and have a quitter's mentality. As a result, they have given up hope on positively influencing their children. They cave in under pressure and allow their children to be influenced by others. Passive parents neither engage in purposeful training nor do they plan for their children's future. They always make excuses like "I'm going to allow them to decide what they want to do" or "I don't want to interfere with their lives." Sadly, their children often suffer because of the poor choices they make and the negative consequences of their actions. Our job is to guide our children along the right paths in life. We cannot possess a lackadaisical attitude when it comes to parenting. Neither should we give up, cave in, or quit when we are faced with challenging situations. Quitting is the easy way out.

Training

Parents who train their children in the fear of the Lord take the responsibility for their children. They do not allow the cares of the world to govern their lives. Neither do they isolate their children from everyone and everything. Rather, they are selective of whom they allow their children to associate with. These parents are confident that they are instilling in their sons and daughters the necessary values that will help them make the right decisions in life.

DEVELOPING GOOD PARENTING SKILLS

As parents, we must take the initiative to become educated in order to develop good parenting skills. Sometimes we think we can just wing it with our children, but parenting is a huge responsibility, and winging it won't get the job done. My advice is to gain as much knowledge and understanding as possible. In all thy getting, get understanding (see Proverbs 4:7).

Establish Rules

Depending upon the age of your children, parents should establish specific rules to which each child must adhere. It is frustrating and unrealistic to expect a four-year-old to abide by the same rules as a nine-year-old. Instead, we should be reasonable in what we expect from our children. Rules should be written down clearly in a manner they can understand and hung in a location designated as the discipline/time-out area as a reminder that the rules will be enforced. Our children will not take us seriously if we make rules and never enforce them.

Be Sure They Understand Discipline

When your children break the rules, deal with it immediately if possible. Take them to your designated area of discipline and explain what they did to displease you. Make sure they clearly understand why they are being disciplined. Teach your children God's perspective on their behavior by showing them what the Bible says about disobedience and rebellion. The following are a good start: Deuteronomy 12:28; 1 Samuel 15:23; Proverbs 3:11–12; Ephesians 6:1–3; Colossians 3:20.

Don't Spare the Rod

There is a difference between correction and punishment. Correction is rooted in affection and concern. It is designed to restore honor and focus. Correction implies, *I'm going to show you the right way because I'm concerned about you.* Punishment, on the other hand, is revenge used to satisfy the need for control. It implies, *I'm gonna get you, because it makes me feel better.* Some parents don't believe in spanking, but I do, because the Bible encourages it. Proverbs 29:15 says that discipline gives wisdom. A child left to his or her own devices will always bring shame to his or her parents. However, please know it is dishonorable to spank your children for every little thing they do. Also, be careful not to magnify the offense or misbehavior, as it can be viewed by the child as rejection. Once children feel rejected, in most cases, they will become rebellious.

Eliminate Rebellion

Rebellion should be dealt with immediately. Children should not be allowed to sulk, pout, or throw temper tantrums. Rebellious children grow up to be rebellious adults. As the years go by, that pout will turn into disrespect for laws and other rules and regulations. For example, rebellious adults have difficulty holding a steady job or receiving promotions because they have a problem submitting to their employer or other forms of authority.

Lead by Example

Be a good role model for your children to follow. Children should not have to look outside of the home for heroes to emulate. At a very young age, children are very impressionable. Their brains are like sponges. They soak up everything they see and hear, whether it is positive or negative. They watch their parents very closely and do what they do and say what they say. If you want to see how your children see you, watch them during their playtime. They will act out what they see and experience. When I was growing up, I always heard adults say, "Do as I say, not as I do." To expect our children to do this is very unrealistic. We learn by example.

As I look at my girls, who are all growing up now to be young women, I am thankful they had a godly, virtuous mother to model after. A lot of what they have learned was not always said. It was instilled in them as they watched her example. As parents, we must show our children how a life dedicated to a loving and faithful Father yields a blessed and prosperous life by our example.

Listen

We must listen to our children. They have feelings, too. As adults, we want to be heard and understood, and our children are no different. We cannot assume we have all the answers. Sometimes the answers come out in communication. When children are not allowed to express themselves, they often act out in response to something that they really need to talk about.

We must be available to our children. They should be made to feel that they can talk to us about anything. And as parents, we must patiently listen and be receptive to their thoughts and opinions. We don't have to agree with everything they say (and we won't!), but hear them out and respond patiently in love. Children shut their parents out when they feel all they hear is criticism and chastisement.

Spend Quality Time Together

Make spending time with your children a priority. Although we can easily get caught up in the demands and issues of life, it is vitally important that we take the time to show our children that they are a priority in our lives. While doing homework together, having lunch at their school, and picking them up from band practice are all important, we should also have personal quality time just to hang out with our children. Believe it or not, your children really want to spend time with you.

Taffi had to put this in perspective for me a few years ago. I had my calendar posted in the kitchen so everyone would know my schedule, especially those dates I would be out of town. I was so focused on my calendar, making sure that I was prepared for all my engagements and appointments, that I was gradually phasing out my family time. Taffi had to talk to me and let me know, "Hey, we need you, too." I hadn't considered how it must have felt to see the calendar posted month after month, with what were considered to be significant, important engagements in my life, upon which their names were not written. After talking with Taffi, I knew I had to make some changes. I rearranged my calendar. I continued to post it, but from then on, when the girls checked it, they saw their names. I remember seeing Lauren's smile when she first saw her name as she looked at the calendar. She was excited and pleased that she had her own special times marked for all to see where she and I were going to spend our special time together. Let your children know they are special. Single each of them out as the precious gifts they are to you and your family, and take the quality time to show it.

Attend Church Together

It is important that your children see how valuable your relationship with God is to you. Sunday morning is not a time to send your children off to church with other family members, or on the church van. Make church attendance a routine family event. Remember, a family that prays together, stays together.

TALKING ABOUT SEX

Sex is one of the most avoided topics in parenting! It is surprising to see the number of parents who prefer that their children learn about sex in school or on their own. This is a big mistake, because they are more likely to get into trouble when left on their own. Buying condoms and other methods of birth control is not the answer; neither is relying on someone else to teach them. It is best that our children learn about sex from us. As their parents, we are their primary and most impactful teachers.

I have to admit, talking about sex can be uncomfortable, but we must get over the discomfort because we do not want our children to be misinformed. In our society, many children are dealing with teenage pregnancy and sexually transmitted diseases. And many of them are dying of AIDS simply because they lack knowledge. The truth is, in most cases, many young people are not mature enough to be dating. They are too young and unprepared to handle the sexual temptation that accompanies one-on-one dating. It is disheartening to see parents who willingly allow their children to form compromising relationships with the opposite sex. We must equip our children with good morals and values, based on the Word of God, which will prevent them from adopting the world's standards.

Setting age-appropriate and Word-based boundaries will prevent our children from placing themselves in situations in which they can be easily tempted. For instance, consider allowing them to "group date" rather than "single date" until confident they are equipped to handle sexual temptation. In addition, we should not allow our sons and daughters to listen to music or watch TV shows or movies that encourage heavy petting and promote promiscuity. This opens the door to the mentality that dating is all about heavy petting and sexual intercourse.

Parents, we must teach our young people to control their sexual urges. In addition, we should explain to them what happens to their bodies as they mature. Self-control is vital (1 Thessalonians 4:3–5). I teach my children that their virginity is a treasure. Sex outside of marriage is against God's Word, and there is no such thing as "safe sex." The only safe sex is abstinence.

In addition to teaching, one of the strongest weapons in this battle against sexual immorality is prayer. It is imperative that we pray for the protection of our children. Pray and believe that your children will remain virgins and maintain self-control (Galatians 5:22–23). Also pray that they have a desire to draw closer to the Lord and learn to make wise decisions.

By teaching our children that sex is reserved for marriage and God is glorified and honored through virginity, we greatly decrease the possibility of the negative consequences of fornication.

We also have the weapon of unconditional love. When we show our children the God-kind of love, they will not have to go looking for love in all the wrong places. Instead, they are fulfilled and secure in the kind of love that never fails. Commitment, consistency, discipline, and love are the fundamentals of good parenting.

I encourage you to make it a habit to show your children how much you love them. Set aside time each day to shower them with hugs, kisses, and encouragement. Involve yourself in their lives by asking open-ended questions, such as "What good thing happened to you today?" Then refuse to accept one-word answers! Keep them talking! Let them know you're their biggest fan by supporting their interests and accomplishments. By continually investing your time, energy, and effort, you reinforce your commitment to your children.

Whether you are a single parent, married parent, grandparent, godparent, or guardian, I take this time to personally encourage you as you continue to take on the awesome responsibility of parenthood. There will be times when it seems too hard, but we are not alone. Our loving Father is there to help us. He said He will never leave us or forsake us. When it gets overwhelming, just rest in Him.

As I look at each of my children, I can't imagine my life without them. They are truly gifts from God. No one said parenting would be easy, but we just learn as we go. There is no such thing as a perfect child, so we have to let them live and learn. Even when they stray away, we can always rest in the promise that if we raise them in the ways of God, they will not be lost. As I often say, they are just gathering testimonies. Just continue to speak the Word over their lives in faith. God is faithful to reward our labor of love as we continue to complete our most important assignments in life—our children.

SECTION THREE

WINNING OVER NEGATIVE EMOTIONS

GET OVER IT!

Ignorance and negative emotions are a lethal combination in our lives. Forgiveness is not a feeling, it is a decision.

Hurting people hurt people. This is more than a cliché; it is a truth that can help us identify the pain in our own lives and more effectively deal with people who hurt those around them. Hurt is a negative emotion that can completely take over our lives if we let it. Many times people use their pain as an excuse to be mean, angry, bitter, and unforgiving toward others, but when we hold on to the disappointment and pain of the past, they will only get worse. More importantly, most of the time, we are the ones who end up suffering.

There are a lot of hurting people in the world, many of whom are Christians. Becoming born again does not automatically erase the hurt and pain in a person's heart. While the spirit is re-created through the salvation experience, the soul is not. Wounded emotions require time, a commitment to heal, and a willingness to yield to God's Word in order for them to be eliminated. Combining these things gives us the power to restore a hurting soul.

I believe ignorance and negative emotions are a lethal combination in our lives. A lack of knowledge can cut us off from certain things God wants to do. And being dictated by our emotions creates an access point for the enemy. Feelings can move us away from the will of God, and being hurt is usually the root of the problem.

STICKS AND STONES

You have probably heard the phrase, "Sticks and stones may break my bones, but words will never hurt me!" Well, let's be honest: words do hurt, and they can affect our hearts and souls for a long time. When people lie, disrespect, belittle, and wound us with words, the effects can have a lasting impact. Hurting people are the product of words spoken to them, which have damaged their emotions.

Proverbs 12:18 says, "There is that speaketh like the piercings of a sword: but the tongue of the wise is health." God is saying if you could experience what it feels like to be pierced with a sword, this is the same way words can cut and wound. Words that are rash and harsh can do as much damage internally as an actual knife can to flesh. We must begin to understand how we have been created—our emotional makeup—so we can practice speaking words that heal rather than hurt.

This area of hurt is something that took me a long time to deal with, particularly because there were so many areas of hurt in my own life. There were some situations where I tried to build on a foundation of hurt and it never worked; things always fell apart. Maybe you have been hurt by a friend or family member, on the job, or in the church. Regardless of the situation, God wants to heal you.

Why are feelings of hurt so dangerous? Because they rob us of the blessings God has intended for our lives. Hurt will distort our decisions and cause our view of the world and other people to be negative. Anytime you are harboring hurt, it is stealing *something* from you. And the enemy will always play on it to his advantage. Before you can really move forward, you must get rid of the hurt.

While the potential to be hurt is always going to be present as you interact with people and journey through life, it does not have to affect you if you know how to handle it properly. You can deal with it so that it does not really bother you at all!

RECOGNIZING HURTING PEOPLE

It is not difficult to recognize hurting people. You can detect signs of hurt and emotional pain fairly easily if you pay attention.

First, hurting people are very unpleasant to be around. Have you ever known people who are always negative? Their words, demeanor, and attitude seem to reflect a constant state of dissatisfaction with everyone and everything around them. They are always finding a way to weave the hurts of their pasts into their conversations. I have encountered many people like this, and it is clear that hurt is lurking just beneath the surface of their emotions.

Second, when people are hurting, they tend to be angry not only at others but also with themselves. Their anger usually turns inward and manifests as depression and stress. Consequently, they may have a short fuse or react to people and situations with harsh words. A hurt person may act out on the anger they feel by lashing out at others and trying to inflict the same pain they feel on the world around them.

Because of the anger a lot of hurting people feel, they tend to wear their emotions on their sleeve. Sometimes they do this so you can start a conversation that allows them to tell you about their pain. Hurting people are also extremely sensitive and very defensive. They often feel that they are being attacked, even when this is not the case at all.

The third signpost of a hurting person is bad decision making. It is so important to avoid making decisions when you are hurt because the decisions you make will most likely be wrong. It is unwise to make choices simply to protect our feelings in the heat of the moment rather than in the best interest of our future. Decisions that are made based on hurt feelings can be costly.

When I was growing up, my dad, who was known as Big Dollar, was a no-nonsense type of man. Quite simply, he was emotionally led most of the time. He worked as a police officer. One particular night he called in sick, and a coworker decided to show up at our house because my dad did not come in to work that night. The police officer banged on our door at two o'clock in the morning, and my father was not happy, to say the least! They exchanged words, and, needless to say, my dad gave him a few more moments to leave the property before taking matters into his own hands! The next thing we heard was the squad car squealing off down the street. I am sure my dad would have killed that guy because his emotions controlled his actions. This is how I was raised. My family let our emotions rule our decisions.

Many of us can recall at least one time when we have made the mistake of making a decision based on hurt feelings. Later, we ended up regretting most of those actions. We cannot think clearly, rationally, and objectively when we are hurt, so the best thing to do is to take some time to step away from whatever the situation may be and regain our footing emotionally. Ask yourself, *How is this decision going to affect my life? Am I going to regret this later?* If the answer is yes, it is definitely not the time to move forward with that particular decision.

HOW TO NEVER BE HURT AGAIN

There is a way to never be hurt again, and it is through the Word of God. Isn't it comforting to know God has made provisions for *anything* you may go through in life, including wounded emotions and hurt feelings? Knowing what He has promised opens the door to new emotional realities.

The key is found in Luke 10:19. "Behold, I give unto you power to tread on serpents and scorpions, and over all the power of the enemy: and nothing shall by any means hurt you." The powerful truth Jesus revealed to us here is that we *can* be emotionally invincible! That's a promise. We no longer have to be hurt by others when we know how to skillfully use the Word to take control over our emotions.

We can become people who will not be defeated or remain the victims of hurt. Real destruction in our lives begins on the inside and works its way to the outside, much like success. There will always be people who say and do things to you that have the potential to cut deeply. However, keep your heart and mind protected, using the Word of God as a shield. Meditate on this promise to prevent being hurt by anyone or anything. Realize the authority God has given you! Take authority over the devil and his attempts to damage your emotions. Refuse to be hurt!

I have had to make that decision in my own life, particularly when it came to people saying negative things about me through the media. It used to bother me to no end when my words would be taken out of context, or people would make up things about me and perpetuate media-fueled rumors and assumptions. But I had to come to a point where I could finally make up my mind and say, *You know what? I refuse to allow the negative and even false things said about me to upset me.* I have come to realize that it is the enemy's goal to discredit honorable men and women of God in order to keep the world blinded to the truth found in God's Word.

I don't care if they call me a crook; I have something on the inside of me that makes me emotionally invincible! I am possessed by the Word of God, and when the enemy comes in like a flood, God will raise up a standard against him.

This type of confidence comes only by spending so much time meditating on the Word that it begins to alter the way you look at people and situations that are designed to cause hurt in your life.

God is love, and when His Word becomes engrafted in your spirit and soul, the Spirit of love will begin to push fear-based hurt, rejection, and pain out of your life. You will start looking at those who offend you as hurting people who are in need of love themselves. This will transform the way you deal with hurtful people, and it will also heal you and make you stronger.

There are some specific things you must do in the heat of an emotional attack. First, remind yourself that Jesus experienced the same emotions, only to an even greater degree. But He never allowed His emotions to determine His decisions, even though He was tempted. When you talk about being hurt, Jesus knew very well what that felt like. From the rejection He received from His own people, to having to go through spiritual and physical death, causing temporary separation from God, nothing we could ever go through can compare to what Jesus went through for us. He did not allow the hurt to overtake Him; He prayed and kept moving onward and upward. Knowing He was able to conquer the pain He was feeling gives us the assurance that we, too, can do the same.

When you feel hurt rising inside you, the next thing you have to do is take authority over it. Do not sit there and allow your mind to replay the experience over and over again. Yes, it is a real emotion, and yes, you feel it. But because you feel it does not mean you are to *yield* to it. This is where the power of decision comes in, along with the power of your tongue. Use the Word of God to cast the hurt out of your mind and heart. If you let it linger, it will take root in your heart and begin to affect your decisions and behavior.

Second Corinthians 10:5 says to cast down imaginations and *every* high thing that exalts itself against the knowledge of God. This includes feelings that attempt to dominate our souls and get us to think and act in a way that contradicts the Word. Cast them out by saying, "I take authority over hurt feelings right now in the name of Jesus. I command my soul to line up with the Word of

God. I keep my mind focused on God, and He keeps me in perfect peace." Even if you have to do this several times a day, continue to aggressively cast negative emotions and thoughts down through the power of God's Word.

PERFECTING THE LOVE OF GOD

The answer to overcoming hurt would not be complete without a reminder about the importance of walking in love and allowing the love of God to dominate our mind-set. Hurt is a selfish emotion because it is focused on self-preservation and -protection. When we are hurt, we can only think about what is going on in our world. Everything is about us.

When people are hurt, they are also more likely to hurt others through their words and actions. All this is for the purpose of protecting themselves from being hurt again. It is really simply fear-based.

The Word tells us fear does not come from God. He has delivered us from fear (2 Timothy 1:7; Hebrews 2:14–15). If you are harboring hurt in your heart, you can be certain fear is present, and you must get rid of it. The way to do this is to develop the love of God in your life to such a degree that it flushes fear out of your mind and heart. By exercising this love in your relationships, you become more developed in it.

First John 4:18 says this: "There is no fear in love; but perfect love casteth out fear: because fear hath torment. He that feareth is not made perfect in love." So if you are hurt, know that torment is involved. Think about the last time you were really hurt. Do you remember all the mental and emotional anguish that came with that pain? The memories of what someone did to us can be tormenting by themselves, and they can keep us locked in the past.

But the love of God is well able to overcome anything anyone has ever done to us. If you question whether you have the ability to love the way God does, consider Romans 5:5, which says, "And hope maketh not ashamed; because the love of God is shed abroad in our hearts by the Holy Ghost which is given unto us."

According to the Word, the very same love God possesses toward mankind—the supernatural ability to love people without conditions—has been deposited in us! This is exciting news because it lets us know God has equipped us with the ability to obey the commandment to love others.

Walking in love means forgiving those who have hurt us. This is probably the most difficult step, but it is the most necessary. When we are hurting and walking in unforgiveness, we are destined to carry that pain with us for years. Many times our responses and reactions to people are fear-based. This is because we have strife in our hearts toward them.

Forgiveness is critical to our healing. As I've said many times, unforgiveness is like drinking poison, hoping the person who wronged you dies. But we end up suffering in the end. Receiving forgiveness from God depends on our forgiveness of others. It does not matter what has been done to you or how badly you have been hurt; you *must* forgive.

In Luke 17:3–5, Jesus gave the disciples the instructions concerning forgiveness: "Take heed to yourselves: If thy brother trespass against thee, rebuke him; and if he repent, forgive him. And if he trespass against thee seven times in a day, and seven times in a day turn again to thee, saying, I repent; thou shalt forgive him. And the apostles said unto the Lord, Increase our faith."

Here Jesus said even if someone trespasses against us seven times in one day, it is our responsibility and obligation to forgive that person. The disciples clearly had challenges receiving this because they immediately asked Jesus to increase their faith. They knew forgiveness is not always easy.

The same is true for us today. Forgiveness is definitely not easy, especially when someone has done something terrible to you. But it is necessary. Forgiveness is not a feeling, it is a decision. Many times we have to forgive by faith, believing our feelings will line up with our decision later on; and they always will. But it starts with a decision. We must forgive as an act of our will.

Once you have forgiven, it is important to stop reliving the offense. This is possibly the main reason hurt lingers in our lives. We never really let the situation go. Forgiveness involves completely releasing the situation to God, believing He is more than able to handle it and deal with the other person. If you continue to hold on to what happened, you are delaying your healing.

I often use the example of a boy with a developing scab to illustrate what happens when we keep returning to our hurt, refusing to let it heal. The boy has a bandage over his wound, but he continues to pull the bandage back in order to show everyone what happened to his knee. He would cover the wound and then reveal it, cover it and reveal it, until eventually it was reopened. The same thing happens to us when we rehearse and relive our pain. You must stop nursing the hurt if you ever want to get free from it.

Trying to get even with those who have hurt us will also slow down the healing process. Although it is tempting to consider as we get caught up in those negative emotions, we must choose to diffuse the temptation. We do this by refusing to rehearse the offense in our minds. If we don't, over time we will become consumed with what the person did or said and start focusing on how we can get even.

We cannot refuse to walk in love and expect God to bless us or even vindicate us. Vengeance is His. He said He will repay, not in our time but in His. We must be sure that we continue to sow seeds of love and pray for those who have hurt us. In the midst of praying for them, healing will take place in us.

TAKE UP THE SHIELD OF FAITH AND STOP MAKING EXCUSES

God has equipped us with the necessary weapons of defense against hurt. One of them is the shield of faith mentioned in Ephesians 6:16: "Above all, taking the shield of faith, wherewith ye shall be able to quench all the fiery darts of the wicked."

What is the shield of faith? It is the Word of God. We allow what the Word says to dominate our minds versus meditating on what someone else says or does to us. Any hurtful word or deed perpetrated against you can be classified as a "fiery dart." But if you will keep that Word at the forefront of your thinking and speak it during emotional attacks against your mind, Satan's fiery darts will not be able to penetrate, and no one will be able to hurt you. You can only get hurt if you put down your shield. This happens when we aren't reading the Word of God—negative words and actions are more penetrating.

I want to challenge you to become aggressive about defending your mind against hurt. Make up your mind right now to hold up the shield of faith. Decide to only think what the Word says about the situation. If you don't, the same people and issues will be able to open old wounds. Meditating on God's Word will continue to protect us from future hurt as it heals the wounds from the past.

It is also important to stop making excuses as to why we are so easily hurt. Have you ever known someone like this? Instead of dealing with the issues going on in their hearts, they just make excuses as to why they are the way they are. This only serves the purpose of keeping us locked in an emotional prison.

Listen, every one of us has a story. All of us have gone through some experience in life that has caused us to feel hurt. Whether it was a parent who was abusive or absent, or a spouse who betrayed you, you cannot continue to make excuses for your negative emotions and continue to do nothing to transform your life for the better. It may sound harsh, but we must *get over it!* We must stop wearing our emotions on our sleeves and believe in God's power to heal.

When it comes to dealing with spiritual and emotional attacks against us, there is nothing more powerful than taking communion over those situations. The power of communion is available to us particularly during these times. The communion table is where things are settled. When you partake of the bread and the wine, you release the power of God into every area of your life and activate the life force of God in your soul. Hurt can become a thing of the past, by making a decision to be free from it. Take advantage of the tools God has made available to you so you can be an overcomer in this area. You never have to be hurt again.

KISS THE BLUES GOOD-BYE

What we do with negative emotions determines
whether we ultimately win.

I'll never forget one of the emptiest times in my life. It was
during my battle with depression. Depression had moved in so
slowly and deliberately that it had initially gone unnoticed. I had
accepted over a hundred engagements during that year and I was
preaching and traveling extensively. In addition to that, I was also
still working as an educational therapist, and the weight of counseling the oppressed and depressed patients was taking its toll. I
was constantly giving out of my spirit, but I was not replenishing
it. As a result, I began to feel very empty. My spirit was so void of
the Word that my mind was left vulnerable to attack.

With an empty spirit, seeds of depression, rejection, suicide,
inadequacy, and inferiority began to develop and grow. These
emotions robbed me of fellowship and communion with God.
The attacks overwhelmed me to the point where my spirit felt dis-
abled, and I wasn't able to sense God's presence.

One day, after coming home from work, I pulled the car into
the garage and just sat there for hours. I didn't want to live like
that anymore, so I sat there contemplating how I could end my
life without going to hell. No answer came to me. So I got out of
the car and went in the house. Although I wasn't sensing God's
presence, something within compelled me to push forward.

The simple truth is: no one is immune to experiencing negative emotions. However, what we do with the negative emotions determines whether we move forward or remain stuck in the same place. There are people who permanently take up residence in the land of negative emotions because they never learn how to deal with their feelings. As a result, they fail to reach the destination of peace, prosperity, and joy God has planned for them. This doesn't have to be our story, however; if we can understand how to appropriately handle our emotions, we will be that much closer to experiencing success, freedom, and personal growth.

When dealing with emotions, we must first understand they are real! There is no point in saying we don't feel negative emotions at times, because that simply is not true. I remember feeling empty and oppressed, yet I continued to maintain my heavy schedule and preach around the world. Denying our feelings will not make them go away, and neither will ignoring them. We will definitely experience negative emotions, but how we choose to respond to them will ultimately determine the outcomes in our lives.

There are three components to every person: we are spirit beings who possess souls and live in physical bodies. The soul is comprised of the mind, will, and emotions. It is in our souls that we think thoughts, feel emotions, and make decisions. We've seen that God desires we prosper in our souls (3 John 1:2) because the degree to which our souls prosper determines the quality of our lives in every area. If negative thoughts and feelings rule our emotions, we can be sure this will inhibit our growth in other areas in our lives.

Emotions can be defined as *feelings on the inside, caused by pain or pleasure, designed to move us toward or away from the will of God for our lives.* Please understand, emotions are not *all* bad. In fact, God gave them to us for a reason. Through positive, healthy emotions, we can experience God in deeper, more meaningful ways, and "feel" Him through love, joy, and peace. When the power of God touches our lives, holy emotions are generated. Our feelings can connect us to God and others in profound ways that reflect untold levels of unconditional love, happiness, and contentment.

We are emotional creatures; however, our emotions were never meant to rule us. In fact, Jesus came to *redeem* every person from the curse of being emotionally ruled, which means we do not have to succumb to negative emotions if we don't want to. Allowing feelings to control our thoughts, words, and actions will inevitably drive us to do things that will take us down the wrong path in life.

If you take a look at the latest headlines, talk shows, and television news programs, it becomes abundantly clear that people all over the world are making emotional decisions, destroying not only their lives but the lives of others as well. Emotions are just that powerful when they are not brought under control. We must learn to identify our negative emotions and deal with them in a healthy way, so we can effectively respond to life's pressures and live life to the fullest.

DEPRESSION: ANGER TURNED INWARD

Also known as "the blues," depression is probably one of the most common negative emotions affecting people today. Depression is anger turned inward. We invite this destructive emotion into our minds when we internalize external pressures and fail to allow God to carry those burdens for us. I recall the Lord telling me it was I, not He, who was responsible for the strenuous workload I was under. Had I sought Him before making those decisions, the burden would have been much lighter. Many times, we become "de-pressed" or pressed down under the weight of life due to the choices and decisions we make.

Having worked as a therapist in the mental health field, I can tell you firsthand that depression is extremely common among the general population. And with the many financial, emotional, and professional pressures facing people in today's rapidly changing world, this is not a surprise.

According to the website of the National Institute of Mental Health, depression is the leading cause of disability among Americans between the ages of fifteen and forty-four. Further statistics show that 6.7 percent of the U.S. population (14.8 million adults) is affected by major depression in a calendar year. And in the United States, more women are diagnosed with depression than men—with the average age of onset being thirty-two, for both genders.[1]

Why are so many people depressed? For many, the reason can be attributed to the fact that they choose to focus on the things going on around them. They simply do not know how to handle life's circumstances and situations in a positive manner. As a result, they crumble when crises hit their lives. Not to mention that everywhere we turn are reports of death, mayhem, doom, and gloom. There are always unfortunate headlines about those who killed themselves, their families, or someone else because they felt they had no way out of their situation. Hopelessness and despair can drive people to take drastic measures, and these emotions generally stem from depression that is not addressed.

So how do we deal with the pressures of life, maintain our sanity and emotional well-being, and still thrive in the midst of it all? Well, for those who choose to believe in the overcoming power of God's Word, there is good news: we do not have to remain in the pit of depression and despair. During that empty time in my life, my spirit was void of the Word. Although I knew the Word, I was not meditating on it and spending time in it on a consistent basis. Failure to do this makes it easy for us to believe the lie that God is not there or He is not listening. God will never abandon or forsake us! Jesus said, "Be of good cheer; I have overcome the world!" (John 16:33). Now that's good news! If Jesus said it, it's a done deal. He is letting us know He has *already* defeated anything we face in life, and each of us has the ability to overcome it as well. All it takes is faith in *His* ability, not our own.

SIGNS AND SYMPTOMS

Depression can manifest itself in different ways, and everyone deals with it differently. When people are depressed, they may feel as if the weight of the world is on their shoulders—to the point where it seems to be crushing the very life out of them. Or there may be a sense of hopelessness and despair that just won't go away.

Depression can overtake a person's life when he or she cannot see any light at the end of the tunnel. The problem worsens when we do not take control over negative thoughts that come into our minds. Further, if we don't know how to handle negativity, pressure, and circumstances, we may find ourselves defenseless against the attacks of the enemy.

With the overwhelming deluge of emotions depression can evoke, many cope with them by turning to alcohol, drugs, or other addictive behaviors to escape the negative emotions they feel. These choices only fuel a destructive cycle of behavior that plunges them deeper into a black hole of anger and discouragement. Some of the warning signs of depression include:

- A nagging sense of despair or hopelessness that won't go away

- Anti-social behavior

- A desire to sleep all the time

- Engaging in self-destructive behavior

- Suicidal thoughts

These are just a few symptoms of depression that, if not dealt with, can lead to serious consequences.

The only failproof way to counteract the blues is to cut off what is causing the onset of depression in our lives and fill our hearts and minds with God's love and His Word. Depression carries with it a sense of darkness, but God's Word is the light that will make that darkness disappear. We must also surround ourselves with people who speak the right things to us. Willpower alone will not do the job, neither will simply thinking "positively," based upon the world's standards. Depression is a spiritual attack against our souls, and it must be dealt with properly.

First consider the attitude we should have toward the things that tend to cause depression. John 14:1 gives clear instruction on how we should look at trouble and pressure when it attacks us: "Let not your heart be troubled: ye believe in God, believe also in me." We can control how we think and what we allow into our hearts. We can make a decision to reject any negative emotion or thought pattern that tries to creep up on us, and we can choose to trust God's Word instead. Though trouble will come, Jesus is our security. When our confidence is in Him, negative emotions, such as depression, have to go!

It is so encouraging to know Jesus experienced *every* negative emotion we go through. He not only experienced them all, but He also *defeated* them all, which gives us hope and confidence to do the same.

Mark 14:33–34 gives an account of Jesus' experience in the Garden of Gethsemane the night before He was crucified. He was going through so many things at the time, including thoughts of depression. Imagine how you would feel knowing you were about to take on the sins, diseases, and the curse of the entire world—die—and then go through the torments of hell. Jesus did. "And He took with Him Peter and James and John, and began to be struck with terror and amazement and deeply troubled and depressed.

And He said to them, My soul is exceedingly sad (overwhelmed with grief) so that it almost kills Me!" (AMP).

Here we see Jesus overwhelmed by negative emotions to the point that He was terrified, deeply troubled, and even depressed. In fact, He was so sad He said it almost killed Him! Jesus was being pressured on every side and was fighting an inner battle that threatened to overtake His emotions and drive Him out of the Father's will. Yet, in His most emotionally trying hour, He dealt with His emotions immediately by speaking words to cancel those negative thoughts and feelings. Instead of giving in to them, He declared God's will over the situation. He *resisted* the suggestions of the enemy! His Words enabled Him to press forward in God's plan for Him.

Like Jesus, we must also deal with negative emotions by *resisting* them. There is a fight involved when negative thoughts and feelings are bearing down on us. We have to subdue our feelings with our words and refuse to allow them to govern our next move. People have tried to make overcoming depression difficult to understand. But quite simply, you must change the way you think if you are going to change the way you feel.

The second thing Jesus did during those critical moments was fall on His face and *pray*. We cannot underestimate the power of prayer when our emotions are going haywire. Jesus did not allow His depression to stop Him from doing what He *knew* to do. Talk to God when you feel struck with negative emotions, when fear, discouragement, and depression come around. When those emotional symptoms show up in your life, that's when you need to pray. If you don't talk to God, you leave room for your emotions to drown out His voice.

Our souls must be subject to our spirits. When the spirit man is in control, it overrides the negative feelings we may be experiencing at any given time. Speaking the Word of God in the midst of the pressure is what activates the authority over our spirit, mind, will, and emotions.

SPEAK TO YOUR FEELINGS!

Did you know you have the power to *speak* to your feelings and they *must* obey you? The psalmists knew this and practiced it. In Psalm 42, the writers actually spoke to their souls and declared positive words over them. Verse 5 says, "Why art thou cast down, O my soul? And why art thou disquieted in me? Hope thou in God: for I shall yet praise him for the help of his countenance."

We must never underestimate the power of words when dealing with our emotions. Words shape the way we think and, subsequently, how we feel.

When battling depression, you must first identify how it got into your life and then deal with it the same way it came in. Because my spirit was void of the Word, I opened the door for emotional sickness to come in, and depression got inside me. One day Taffi came and said to me, "Baby, you need to get away. I am getting you away from here. We're going to take a vacation."

It was during that time that I shut myself in a hotel room. It was just God and me. When I started praying, it seemed as though I had been praying for three hours, but it had only been ten minutes. That's how empty I was. So I started again, and I made it to an hour. That's when I heard the Lord. He said, "I want you to take my Word over every issue in your life and speak it aloud any time the attacks of depression come against you." And every time I'd sense those negative thoughts or feelings, I'd take out the Word and start reading it aloud. I would read about fifty specific Scriptures. And I confessed that Word; sometimes I read those Scriptures twenty times a day. I began to notice that each day I required less reading time on those particular Scriptures. And then came the breakthrough. I remember the day it started—joy overflowed within my soul. Joy was mine. Peace was mine. My strength was renewed. And I said, "Whew! God, I'm ready!"

We know depression comes from the outside in. So if we are

having a bout with depression, the first thing to examine is the words we are speaking and listening to, and then change those words. Are we paying attention to negative words coming from an outside source? The words we hear will form pictures in our minds that fuel our imaginations. Maybe our friends and family are telling us things that are only reinforcing a spirit of depression in us. Or it could be we are listening to words being spoken to our minds by the enemy of our souls—Satan. Our own conscience can speak to us as well. And if it is being influenced by the world's news, thoughts, ideas, and attitudes, we will tell ourselves things that will only make us feel worse.

Winning over depression requires an active strategy that includes changing the things we are looking at and listening to, resisting and casting negative words out of our minds, and putting the *right* things in our hearts and minds on a consistent basis.

If you think about it, the world is always pumping news of doom and gloom through every available media outlet. If you don't do anything to combat it, it won't be long before it gets inside you. Getting the upper hand on depression may mean removing yourself from people and environments that are feeding those negative feelings. If you cannot get out of your immediate environment, make it a point to constantly fill yourself with words that uplift and strengthen you. Listen to music that will lift your spirit. Listen to CDs and watch DVDs with anointed praise and worship and sound biblical teaching. Guard your eyes and ears. Keeping your mind and spirit full of God's Word is critical.

Recognize that when pressures come, this is not the time to stand there and be still. Speaking the Word of God is always an effective tool for defeating negative thoughts and emotions like depression. When you quote a Scripture in response to a negative thought intruding on your mind, you cast negative thoughts down. The more you do this, the more you form a protective barrier against negative emotions like depression.

You cannot fight thoughts with thoughts, only with words.

When a negative thought comes to you, you have to open your mouth and say something. When you feel depressed, instead of just wallowing around in the negative emotion, allowing it to press you deeper into despair, declare what God says about you. Words are powerful, and the moment you release them in faith, you affect your body, soul, and spirit in a positive or negative way.

Every day I speak positive, faith-filled words. From the day I broke free up to this very day, the spirit of depression has not been able to infect me. I've had many opportunities. Persecutions, accusations, and hurts still come, but depression can't get in. I know what to say. I get those same Scriptures out and get right on them again. It is the Word that saves my soul and strengthens me.

Mark 14:35 gives further insight into defeating depression when it attacks your mind: "And he went forward a little, and fell on the ground, and prayed that, if it were possible, the hour might pass from him." When Jesus faced depression, He continued to move "forward." Becoming paralyzed is the worse thing you can do when depression is trying to overtake you. You *must* keep going in the direction you know God wants you to go, no matter how you feel. Momentum is the key. When you stop moving, it is easier for the enemy to keep you bound. We must choose to trust God and keep moving in His direction.

STEPS TO GET OUT OF DEPRESSION

If you are already in a depressed state of mind, it can be difficult to pull yourself out. But here are some key steps to take to start the process.

Step One: Guard Your Heart

Be conscious at all times of what you are allowing in your spirit via the things you are looking at, listening to, and talking about.

The eyes, ears, and mouth are the three gateways to the heart that allow seeds of despair to become planted within you. You have control over what you allow to trouble your heart, based on what you believe. Choose not to be troubled by *anything* and, instead, trust God.

Step Two: Speak to Your Problems

Speak *to* your problems rather than speaking *about* them. What you rehearse will reinforce its reality in your life. Mark 11:23 says we should speak to our mountains in faith, and they will be removed.

Step Three: Ask God to Meet Your Needs

If something is missing in your life, ask God for it rather than meditating and speaking about your need. Jesus says we should ask the Father for what we need in His name and He will give it to us (John 16:23–24). There is no need to become depressed over lack when God promises to supply the things we need and desire. Not only that, He delights in our prosperity.

Step Four: Be Grateful

After you believe you receive, thank God. Thanksgiving and praise always defuse depression! Praise stops the enemy in his tracks; it paralyzes him. Find something, anything, to praise God about, and the spirit of depression will begin to leave.

Because we become so consumed with everything that *seems* wrong in our lives, oftentimes depression hinders our ability to keep things in proper perspective or hear God clearly. However, circumstances and situations in life are temporal, meaning they are subject to change. Attacks of depression are just the enemy's attempts at getting you to focus on problems rather than look to

God. Chase your blues away by praising God and thinking about how good He has been to you. Fill yourself with the Word of God and only speak positive, faith-filled words. When you consistently do these things, you will never be subject to another day of depression. Sure, things will happen; that's life. But make up your mind to use the tools God has given you to defend your mind against negative emotions, and kiss the blues good-bye.

THE INFERIORITY COMPLEX THAT STOPS US

God has given each of us unique qualities. Discover and gain confidence in these things.

There is a monster lurking in the hearts and minds of people everywhere. This monster hinders us from reaching levels of contentment and joy that we have a right to. It causes us to compare ourselves to others and completely discount our unique purposes in life. *Inferiority* is its name, and it is a negative emotion that destroys lives and relationships. If we can begin to look at ourselves honestly and deal with this emotional monster, we can start enjoying and appreciating who we are, without reservation. Our relationships with those around us will greatly improve as well.

Have you ever met someone who had an inferiority complex? I think all of us have areas in our lives where we may have felt inferior at some point. It may be our physical appearance, educational background, or personal abilities. We look at ourselves and then we look at other people and we begin to compare. Without realizing it, we slowly begin chipping away at our self-worth and start looking for ways to compensate for the deficiencies we perceive in ourselves.

Those who feel inferior *always* compare themselves to others and never feel they quite measure up. Like a cancer, feelings of inferiority poison us and cause a persistent sense of inadequacy. Inferior people often feel powerless, small, and unimportant.

Because of this, they usually spend the majority of their lives trying to prove something to others, all because they feel they fall short in some area of their lives.

There are many reasons why people feel inferior. Childhood trauma, personal life experiences, and other circumstances can plant seeds of inferiority in our hearts. If never dealt with and uprooted, these feelings of inadequacy will continue to influence our motives and actions. We will continue to feel frustrated and powerless, and we will act out in ways that damage ourselves and those around us. Inferiority has to be understood and dismantled in order for us to truly experience emotional freedom and peace within ourselves, no matter what stage of life we are in.

Like all other negative emotions, inferiority originated from Adam and Eve's disobedience in the Garden of Eden. When they sinned, by eating the fruit of the forbidden tree, they opened themselves up to serious consequences. They disconnected themselves from the life of God and connected themselves to the spirit of fear, which brought with it sickness and death.

Being emotionally ruled was a part of that curse Adam and Eve received in the earth. They went from being ruled by the Spirit of God to being ruled by negative emotions. Everything became darkened and twisted because of their sin, including the emotions God gave them. Instead of having uninterrupted fellowship with God, they became consumed with self-preservation. They lost God-consciousness and became *self*-conscious.

When you really think about it, isn't that what inferiority is about? Self-consciousness turns our attention to *our* issues, our failures, and our concerns, rather than focusing our attention on how we can bless others. It is all about how *we* look in the eyes of other people, and whether we are measuring up to a standard God did not necessarily set. It causes us to become ungrateful and self-centered.

When a person feels inferior, there is something wrong in the emotional realm. Such was the case with Adam, after he and Eve missed the mark. His emotions became distorted and he hid from God instead of running to Him. All of a sudden, this man, who once had confidence, pleasure, and assurance while fellowshiping with God, was found cowering behind bushes. Because of sin, negative emotions such as inferiority were allowed to creep in.

WHAT'S ON THE INSIDE MUST COME OUT

Happiness and contentment start on the inside. If we aren't happy with ourselves, we will not be happy with anyone else. It doesn't matter how great our spouses, friends, and loved ones are. When we feel bad about ourselves, that inner image will spill over into everything we do. Unhappy people, who are dissatisfied with themselves, find it difficult to rejoice with those who obtain happiness and success. Inferior people have a hard time demonstrating excitement over others' accomplishments because they are too busy comparing themselves to them or trying to outdo them.

Romans 3:23 says something very interesting: "For all have sinned, and come short of the glory of God." This Scripture gives an account of how all who believe in Jesus can be made righteous—because *all* have sinned and come short of the glory of God. In other words, the opportunity for salvation is available to *every* person who will receive it because we were all born into sin as a result of Adam's mistake in the garden. But there is something else we can glean from this Scripture that sheds light on this whole issue of inferiority.

Because of the fall of man, we all fail to measure up to the glory. The word "glory" here in this context means to become all that God originally intended you to be. The term "come short of" means to be inferior.

Now if we put these definitions together properly, the Scripture would read like this: "Because of sin, we have all become inferior to what God originally intended for us to be." Therefore, many of the weaknesses and problems in our lives stem from inferiority. It is an emotional issue, caused by sin, that leads many to a defeatist mentality that says, "I don't really feel I'll ever be good enough." This way of thinking is a result of the curse.

This inferiority complex is something that starts inside people and works its way out, through the way they think, talk, and act. It colors their interactions with others in a negative way and sabotages relationships. It breeds self-hatred and low self-esteem. It is the mind-set that tells people to go out and alter the way they look to compete with man-made physical standards. It is the spirit behind competitive jealousy and a host of other emotional problems. When people feel inferior inside, it will eventually be seen on the outside.

After God called me into the ministry, I struggled for years with an inferiority complex. I constantly compared myself to other preachers and wondered if I had what it took to be able to do what I was called to do. And you know what? I just got so tired of all that and finally said, *Here's what I'm going to do: I'm just going to be the best me I know how to be because I don't know how to be all those other people.* I had tried to be all of them. It wasn't until I was okay with the way God made *me*—from my personality to my teaching style—that I began to experience freedom from inferiority. It started on the inside and worked its way to the outside.

THE PATTERN OF INFERIORITY

Inferiority progresses from one point to the next, taking us further into a negative emotional rut. It flows like this:

1. *Sin* causes us to fall short of God's approval. When we are not in right relationship with God, it causes condemnation. We feel as if we have *fallen short*.

2. *Falling short* produces overwhelming inferiority. We constantly rehearse our faults and shortcomings in our minds. We see ourselves as people who just cannot measure up in different areas. Once inferiority reaches this stage, it opens the door to more *negative emotions* such as insecurity, jealousy, and pride—a false sense of superiority.

3. *Negative emotions*, stemming from inferiority, now give birth to a feeling of powerlessness, which causes depression and anger. Because they feel powerless, angry people often use their anger to manipulate others.

Inferiority breeds a spirit of control. Its driving force motivates us to rule over others rather than serve them. When we feel inferior, we are intimidated by the things we are supposed to have dominion over. As children of God, we should focus on taking authority over our flesh and the issues that come against us in the physical realm. However, this does not mean we should try to exert our authority, attempting to manipulate and dominate others.

In Luke 10:19, the Word says we have dominion over the enemy and everything he throws at us. We also have dominion over the resources of the earth and everything in it. These are the areas God wants us to dominate.

When Taffi and I got married, I had to realize the covenant we entered into was not about my dominating her or making her feel inferior because of *my* inferiority issues. I didn't have the right to rule her with an iron fist because I felt inferior.

A lot of men struggle with feelings of inferiority and it ends up playing out in their marriages. But in a marriage relationship, there is no room for inferiority complexes. Both the husband and wife must allow the character of God to dominate them so they can be a blessing to each other. It will be virtually impossible to have healthy, happy relationships if the feelings of inferiority we carry are not addressed. We have to start creating new patterns in our lives and change our thinking so we can change the way we feel about ourselves.

SIGNS OF AN INFERIORITY COMPLEX

There are definitely some clear signs of inferiority that can help us to locate where we are and realize that we need to make adjustments in this area. First, inferiority produces an attitude of false superiority. It causes us to carry ourselves in a way that says, "I'm better than you." It is an arrogant attitude that really stems from feelings of falling short. Romans 12:3 tells us to avoid thinking more highly of ourselves than we should. People who act as though they are superior to others are really masking feelings of inadequacy they are harboring within themselves.

Second, inferiority causes us to constantly feel the need to impress others and prove to them how great or wonderful we are. The mistake we often make here is forgetting about what *we* have been called to do. We pretend to be something we're not just to impress someone else. This is a clear symptom of inferiority.

Boasting is yet another sign of an inferiority complex. Have you ever met people whose conversations are predominantly about themselves, their accomplishments, and their abilities? I have always been leery of these types of people. When we puff ourselves up by always bragging, it is a clear indication that inferiority is lurking behind the scenes.

Second Corinthians 10:13 says, "We, on the other hand, will not boast beyond our legitimate province, and proper limit, but will keep within the limits [of our commission which] God has allotted us as our measuring line and which reaches and includes even you" (AMP). Instead of trying to brag, we should strive to keep our thinking sober and try not to become high-minded. Sober thinking is even-keeled and has a balanced perspective of self and life.

Along the same lines, inferior people also grudgingly admit their own shortcomings, while they quickly point out those of others. They do this because they already feel inferior, especially in the very areas where they criticize others.

Other signs of inferiority include:

- Being a bully or having no respect for others' boundaries

- Feeling attacked when someone disagrees with us

- Feeling belittled when confronted or receiving correction

- Blaming others for our problems and never taking responsibility for where we are

- Deriving our worth or value from our performance or appearance

- Being touchy, fragile, or easily hurt

- Being critical and defensive

- Finding fault in others in order to make ourselves feel better

THE SOLUTION

If you struggle with inferiority, there is hope! As with any other soul sickness, God has made a way of escape, and His answer frees us forever. The blood of Jesus has destroyed the inferiority complex and every negative emotion that is born out of it.

Knowing what the blood of Jesus has accomplished for us is the first step toward eradicating this destructive emotion. Traditional religion references the blood of Jesus, but a lot of people really do not know *how* the blood is relevant to their everyday issues and struggles. Awareness, knowledge, and understanding of it are critical to walking in freedom and deliverance.

When we understand what the blood of Jesus has accomplished, we gain confidence in our ability to go to God at any time, knowing He accepts us with open arms. The blood of Jesus allows us to enter God's presence without guilt, condemnation, or inferiority. We can ask for help in a time of trouble and rest assured that He hears and answers our prayers.

Because we have an Advocate who pleads our case before the Father, we know "if we confess our sins, he is faithful and just to forgive us our sins, and to cleanse us from all unrighteousness (1 John 9). Through the blood of Jesus, we can have soundness in our spirits and souls, as well as in our bodies. When we pray, instead of going to God and saying, "Lord, I'm not worthy to get answers to my prayers, and I feel as if I've fallen short," we can say, "I have a blood-bought right to come boldly before the throne of God to pray and get answers! I've got a right!"

Through our gifts and talents alone, we fall short, but in Him we can do all things! When we tell ourselves there is something we cannot do or achieve, it is like saying Jesus cannot do all things. Jesus destroyed the curse of being emotionally ruled, which includes succumbing to feelings of inferiority. When we are in relationship with Him, we look at ourselves through His eyes and see ourselves differently. We don't feel the need to compete with or compare ourselves to others. We have confidence in the wonderful gifts, talents, and abilities God has given to us and appreciate those we see in others. In essence we are happy with ourselves. In Him we not only live, move, and have our being, but we also have confidence.

To live a life free of inferiority and full of God's love, take the following steps:

Step One: Discover and Follow God's Plan for Your Life

Philippians 2:13 says, "For it is God which worketh in you both to will and to do of his good pleasure." God is working in us and energizing us! All we have to do is surrender our will to Him and follow His plan for our lives.

Step Two: Develop Self-Esteem by the Measure of God

God's measure is the love measure. But when you find an inferior person, you will also find a person who is selfish. Stop comparing yourself to others and belittling yourself! Take your focus off yourself and look for ways to bless other people.

Step Three: Place Yourself at God's Disposal

Every day make your gifts and abilities available for His use. By doing this, you open your life to all God has for you.

Step Four: Close Your Mind to False Hopes

Give up visions of grandeur. Be realistic about where you are at this point in your life and what you can do with the resources that are currently available to you.

The most important thing to remember is, regardless of how you may perceive yourself and your abilities, God's response to inferiority is: "It doesn't make a difference who you are; I am all you need." You may have reservations about doing what you are called to do, but remind yourself *God is all you need*. When you start feeling inferior at times, just say, *You know what? God, who is my Source, is all I need*. When the deal hasn't gone through yet, when five years have come and gone and you still have not met Mr. or Ms. Right, just remind yourself of this simple truth. Your appreciation will expand your opportunities.

Step Five: Be Conscious and Appreciative of the Gifts God Has Given You

Each of us possesses unique qualities no one else has. Discovering and gaining confidence in these things set us free from the trap of comparisons.

Step Six: Know Who You Are and What Authority God Has Given You

Revelation 1:6 says, "And [He] hath made us kings and priests unto God and his Father; to him be glory and dominion for ever and ever. Amen." You've been made a king! Now think about how a king carries himself. He knows who he is and he knows his position. He does not question what he can and cannot do because kingship carries with it certain privileges. He makes rules, sets laws in motion, and judges situations. He has abilities that are recognized and respected by others. He is not in competition with people because he knows who he is.

The key to defeating inferiority is embracing who we are. As children of the King, we willingly serve others because we are confident in our God-given lineage. It is only the guy who doesn't understand that he has *already* been made a king who tries to maintain an attitude of superiority—and finds serving others difficult. But when you know who you are and *whose* you are, you get rid of the false pretenses and walk in God's love.

Now is the time to adopt a kingly mentality and declare the inferiority complexes in our lives defeated. God has invested power and ability in each of us, but we have to *know* it. Living with an awareness of who we really are in Him will eliminate any feelings of inadequacy and enable us to maximize the unique gifts we possess inside.

SELF-DOUBT: A HINDRANCE TO YOUR PROGRESS

Remembering always what God has done for us—not what we have done for Him—is the ultimate confidence builder.

If there ever was a negative emotion responsible for absolutely paralyzing our progress in life, self-doubt would fit the bill. Self-doubt attacks our ability to live productive and successful lives by causing us to become unstable in our faith. Everything in God's system operates by faith, but when self-doubt enters our minds and hearts, it shuts down our ability to stand on the Word of God with confidence.

What do I mean when I say *self-doubt*? Whom am I describing? Simply put, it is the person who doubts himself, his abilities, who he is in Christ, and what his purpose is. It is the guy who questions himself all the time. He operates in *questioning* rather than confidence.

Questioning is different from asking God a question. For example, when Mary received word from the angel that she would conceive a child without having sex with a man, she asked, "How can this be?" Mary's question was legitimate because the instructions she received defied natural laws. It is not physically possible, in the natural, to have a child without having sex, or without the sperm of a man. In spite of not understanding how God would do it, Mary took the angel at his word and believed what he told her. Her question did not cause doubt and unbelief, but rather it helped strengthen her faith because of the answer God gave her.

On the other hand, when John the Baptist was imprisoned by King Herod, he started to question God rather than trust Him. Keep in mind, John was Jesus' first cousin, and he had heard the audible voice of God declare Jesus as the Son of God. However, during his time in prison, John saw his negative emotions begin to get the best of him. And instead of holding on to what he knew God said, which could have opened the door to his deliverance, he became offended because Jesus had not come to get him out of jail. As a result, he began to doubt if Jesus even was who God said He was!

Matthew 11:2–3 says, "Now when John had heard in the prison the works of Christ, he sent two of his disciples, and said unto him, Art thou he that should come, or do we look for another?" What John was essentially asking was, "You're supposed to be the Son of God, but why haven't you shown up to help me?" *Questioning* is evidence of doubt, and doubt will stop us from receiving from God. You can see this with people who say, "Well, if God is really God, why did this happen?" They are not really asking *why* it happened; it is more so that they feel as if the tragedy *shouldn't* have happened. As a result, they begin to doubt whether God's love and power are real.

If you wonder if you are doubting, examine the questions that keep coming up concerning the things you are going through, and even the spiritual disciplines in your life. For example, you may be feeling that when you are praying, you should be reading your Bible. Or when you are reading your Bible, you ask yourself, *Should I be praying?* Perhaps you feel that when you are sleeping you should be up doing something else. Or if you are married, you may wonder if maybe you should be single or vice versa. Self-doubt is a constant state of ambivalence about what you are doing and where you are in life.

Although we know what the Word says, self-doubt creates

doubt and fear in certain areas of our lives. It causes us to question whether the Word is really our final authority. It absolutely paralyzes faith.

When we are in self-doubt, we are really being double-minded. We are vacillating between two different ways of thinking— our emotions and intellect versus what the Word says. And this double-mindedness leads to unstable lives. James 1:8 says a double-minded man is unstable in not just some of his ways, but *all* of his ways. When doubt is present in our hearts and minds, it limits our ability to focus on hearing and receiving from God.

AN ATTACK ON OUR CONFIDENCE

Self-doubt is a direct attack on our confidence. Being double-minded only serves the purpose of weakening our faith. And once our faith is weakened, we have nothing on which to stand.

Because faith is a practical expression of our confidence in God and His Word, the enemy is always looking for ways to undermine that confidence. Doubt is one of the primary strategies he uses. Satan's objective is to get us to start questioning the things we see in the Word, the things God has spoken and shown us, the call of God on our lives, and all the things we once knew for sure came from God. All it takes is one suggestion or thought to get us wondering whether what God said is really true. It is deception at its finest.

Please understand, the enemy does not want us to have confidence in what Jesus did for us. He doesn't want us to believe we have been made righteous by the blood of Jesus or that we have a right to be forgiven for our sins. He especially wants us to doubt God's love for us because we will then begin to run away from God instead of *to* Him when we miss the mark.

Hebrews 10:35 tells us why confidence is so important: "Cast not away therefore your confidence, which hath great recompense of reward." Confidence is guaranteed to cause a return in your life if you refuse to let it go. It has *compensation* attached to it. In light of this fact, it makes sense that the enemy does everything he can to attack this crucial area of our faith walk. He does not want us to have confidence in our prayers, in the Word of God, or in what God has said about us.

Self-doubt comes as a result of what I call "taking the second thought." It occurs when we accept the contradiction to God's Word and begin to meditate on it more than we do on what God says. Once that thought is given place in our minds, we become vulnerable to double-minded thinking.

A great example of self-doubt and its effects is found in the account of Peter walking on water. Like Jesus, he demonstrated how to defy natural laws through faith and confidence. However, the moment his faith wavered, self-doubt entered his mind and he began to sink.

And Peter answered him and said, Lord, if it be thou, bid me come unto thee on the water. And he said, Come. And when Peter was come down out of the ship, he walked on the water, to go to Jesus. But when he saw the wind boister-ous, he was afraid; and beginning to sink, he cried, saying, Lord, save me. And immediately Jesus stretched forth his hand, and caught him, and said unto him, O thou of little faith, wherefore didst thou doubt? (Matthew 14:28–31)

Peter believed God enough to step out of the boat and do what he saw Jesus doing. But he began to pay attention to the circum-stances around him. The wind and the waves distracted him and weakened his faith. Can you imagine what thoughts were going through his mind when he began to see the roughness of the sea and the strong winds blowing? *Look at these waves; you could sink at any moment.* Peter accepted those thoughts and took his eyes off Jesus. He began to doubt himself—and God. His confidence was disrupted and he began to sink.

Adam and Eve also compromised what God told them by taking a second thought in the Garden of Eden. When the enemy came in and told Eve she would be like God by eating of the forbidden fruit tree, she fell for the contradictory suggestion. Even though she and Adam had already received a word from God and instructions about how to govern themselves in the garden, they allowed another way of thinking to infiltrate their minds. As a result, they disobeyed God and disconnected themselves from the blessing. The enemy stole their confidence in what God said by planting seeds of doubt in their minds.

The same is true in our own lives. How many times have we set out to do something with great excitement and confidence, but as soon as we looked at what was going on around us, our strength failed? We decided to do something that seemed impossible, or something that took a lot of faith to accomplish, but became distracted by outside influences.

When God spoke to me about starting World Changers Church International and gave me a vision of the World Dome where we now hold our weekly services, I had moments of self-doubt. It was hard for me to conceive how it would all come to pass. I didn't consider myself the most qualified person for such a task, nor did I understand exactly how to go about doing what God told me to do. Self-doubt did rear its ugly head, but I had to continue to trust God every step of the way. Now that I am experiencing the results of my faith, I can see why the enemy tried to get me to doubt the vision God gave me. Even though it was difficult at times, I had to stay focused on what God told me. I had to overcome double-mindedness and believe what God said about what He had called me to do.

Not everyone is called to start a church, but there is something God has told each of us to do that will require faith. What circumstances are causing you to doubt what you desire to do? Maybe the finances aren't exactly what you would like them to be, so you begin telling yourself you cannot accomplish your goals.

Or you may feel you do not have the background, education, or experience to perform a certain calling or undertaking. If we start focusing on all the natural circumstances that contradict our faith, we can easily become double-minded and remain where we are, never progressing forward. We become paralyzed in the grip of self-doubt. It all happens when we take the second thought, choosing to abandon what God says in favor of the contradiction.

So how do we hold on to our confidence when everything around us screams failure and impossibility? How do we remain single-minded about the things we want to do in life when circumstances, personal shortcomings, and negative thoughts try to distract us from goals, dreams, and purpose? The answer is simple: by focusing our minds wholeheartedly on God and keeping our thoughts *fixed* on His Word. He is our confidence.

Remembering always what God has done for us—not what we have done for Him—is the ultimate confidence builder. As I think about this concept, the old gospel hymn "Count Your Blessings" comes to mind. I believe counting our many blessings and the wonderful things God has done is really a tried and true key to having confidence in God. Take a moment to think about all the things He has done for you up to this point. Reflect on the many situations He has brought you out of and how His mercy showed up time and time again, even when you did not deserve it. Has He ever let you down?

It may sound like a cliché, but what we think about on a consistent basis really does determine our course in life. Words determine our thoughts, and thoughts determine how we feel. Self-doubt is a negative emotion, and in order to defeat it we must keep our minds set on the right things at *all* times. The mind is the place where the emotional battles we face are won or lost.

You may be saying, "Brother Dollar, I hear you, but no one can keep his mind on God all the time. I mean, come on, you just can't really control what you think about." Actually, this line of thinking is far from the truth. You *can* control your thoughts and you *can* choose what you will think about on a daily, hourly, and even moment-to-moment basis.

Maintaining a positive thought life is going to be the key to mental victory when it comes to self-doubt. Since everything begins with our mind-sets, we must first determine that we will not allow negative thoughts and emotions to overtake us. Next comes the part most people are not willing to do. We must be disciplined in guarding our minds and casting down negative thoughts when they occur.

A simple exercise you can do to practice casting down thoughts is to count to ten in your mind. Somewhere between one and ten, say your name out loud. What happened to your silent mental count? It was interrupted by the word you spoke. This is the way we cast down negative thoughts when they arise. When a thought comes that says, *I don't think I can do this*, open your mouth and say, "I can do *all* things through Christ who strengthens me!" Any time we find ourselves being double-minded, we have to recognize it as an attack of self-doubt. Then we have to speak what God says so we can immediately eliminate those negative thoughts and get on with the business of keeping our minds on God. The more we practice capturing thoughts, the more we will find ourselves able to maintain our mental focus on God's Word.

The Lord promises something that I have grown to appreciate and found to be so true: when we keep our minds on Him, He will keep us in *perfect* peace. Not just peace, but *perfect* peace. This is why He wants us to reject thoughts of self-doubt. Negative emotions disrupt fellowship with the Father and cause us to get into an emotional arena that renders our faith ineffective. If we *feel* we cannot do something or that God is mad at us, this line of thinking will affect our productivity. This "perfect" peace God is talking about here involves our wellness and our security in every area of our lives. This peace gives us calm that is unaffected by circumstances.

Double-minded thinking can also take place when our souls

are not under complete subjection to God and His Word. But we can choose, as an act of our will, to keep our thinking sober and aligned with God's perfect peace. Self-doubt cannot get in when we have already set our minds to focus on the good things God says about who we are and what we can do—through Him.

When Jesus was tempted in the wilderness by Satan, the attempt of the enemy was to get Him to doubt He was the Son of God! Matthew 4:1–4 describes what happened and how Jesus handled this situation.

> Then was Jesus led up of the Spirit into the wilderness to be tempted of the devil. And when he had fasted forty days and forty nights, he was afterward an hungred. And when the tempter came to him, he said, If thou be the Son of God, command that these stones be made bread. But he answered and said, It is written, Man shall not live by bread alone, but by every word that proceedeth out of the mouth of God.

Satan's attack was on Jesus' mind and His confidence. Satan's plan was to plant self-doubt in Jesus. Jesus *knew* what He had come to the earth to do. He had a goal and a vision that He was focused on accomplishing. Satan's goal was to get Jesus to take a second thought. But Jesus turned the tables on him by speaking words to keep His thinking on track. By responding to Satan with the Word of God, He shut down the negative suggestion and maintained His peace. He kept His mind on what the Word said and rejected the voice of the devil.

STARVE YOUR DOUBTS!

If you struggle with self-doubt, you can be rid of it for good. Following this outline will have you well on your way to victory.

Believe the Love God Has for You

When we believe God's love, we are assured things will work out for our good. When we know God loves us, we know the outcome is secure. Belief in the love of God pumps up our confidence. Sometimes we have to remind ourselves how much we are worth to God. We were fearfully and wonderfully made in the image of Him who created us. He knows the very number of hairs on our heads. We are the apple of His eye. When we are sure of God's love for us, we know He always supplies our needs. When we are in pain, we know we are already healed. When we are in trouble, we know victory is assured. With this confidence, we can conquer the world!

Stop Second-Guessing Yourself and Do What God Tells You to Do

When Peter was about to step out of the boat and walk on the water, he said to Jesus, "If it is you, ask me to come to you." When Jesus said, "Come," that was all Peter needed to hear. By simply hearing Jesus' invitation to come, Peter knew he was talking to the Savior, and he trusted Him. Initially, his faith and confidence in Jesus were all that was necessary for him to step out of the boat and succeed at walking on the water.

Anytime you receive a spoken Word from God, it is always equipped with the provision necessary to support what He said to do. Do not second-guess, doubt, or question how everything is going to work out. Just trust God. Put your confidence in the absolute infallibility of what He says.

Stop Condemning Yourself

Since we know taking the second thought causes self-doubt, we have to be sure to deal with the second thoughts in life. Most of us have experienced what it is like to decide to stand on the Word of God and, later, hear that second thought. The yielding to temptation stops the faith process. As we give an ear to those opposing thoughts, we begin to question God.

When you hear something like, "God is mad at you for what you did," or you have a persistent feeling of condemnation, it is clear you are hearing thoughts that are not coming from the Spirit of God. Cast those thoughts down by speaking what God has said about you. *Any* thought that does not line up with the Word must be checked at the door.

RENEW YOUR MIND

Self-doubt can become a mind-set that is so ingrained in your thinking that you constantly sabotage your development in life. We must renew our minds for victory if we are to ever get beyond limited thinking. I can say from experience that constantly meditating on what God says is essential to obtaining and maintaining a sound mind.

I had to examine every area in my life where I was experiencing self-doubt. While considering both my ministry and my relationships, God spoke to me and said, "You've got to meditate on the answer so that when those negative thoughts return, they simply won't have any effect on your mind."

You have got to train yourself in thinking a different way about yourself. And it is not what you do one time that is going to get results. It is what you are willing to do for a lifetime. I had to say to myself, *Even if the crowds get smaller, I am already ready for that. My confidence in what God has called me to do has nothing to do with how many people show up for church. Even if no one shows up, I'm still going to preach! My confidence is in God's ability, not my own.*

It is time to start doubting our doubts and feeding our faith. Imagine what the devil would do if we started doubting what *he* has to say to us. In fact, I dare you to talk back to the enemy the next time a thought of self-doubt comes in your mind, and say, "No, devil, I doubt what you're saying will come to pass. You may try to get me to buy the lie, but I doubt it. I believe God!" Turn his weapons back on him and see what happens.

Nothing else equips us with the tools we need to overcome negative thinking and emotions except the Word of God. It is the foundation for our success, and success begins with the way we think. Renewing our minds takes place as we spend considerable time in that Word—pondering it, applying it to our lives, and aligning our thinking with it. The more we renew our minds, the more we will begin to see ourselves as God sees us, and our confidence in Him will soar. We will find ourselves walking securely, free from doubt and double-mindedness.

I encourage you to receive the revelation of your worth and value today, by faith. Be reminded that when your confidence is in God, you can rest in what He says to you and about you. Just as Peter walked on the water, you, too, can conquer the circumstances around you and rise to a higher level of results in your life. Renounce self-doubt and the second thought, and declare your faith has endurance that gets the job done every time.

NO CONDEMNATION

Continue to walk in the love of God in order to remain free from the law of sin and death.

Have you ever done something that left you feeling God was mad at you or you were a terrible person? Do you persistently feel unworthy or undeserving of good things? These feelings stem from condemnation, a negative emotion that keeps us from receiving God's love for us. It leaves us hopeless and steals our vision so we cannot see or imagine the wonderful future God has in store for our lives.

I began to think about this whole issue of condemnation and the awesome power of God's love. I thought about how so many people believe God hates them, some believing they have passed the point of no return: His mercy, love, and forgiveness are no longer available to them. Condemnation, stemming from sin-consciousness and misunderstanding the righteousness of God, truly wreaks havoc in the lives of many people—causing them to shy away from His goodness.

The word *condemn* means "to judge unfit for use."[1] A good illustration of this concept is a building that has been condemned or declared no longer fit for occupancy. It is the house with boarded windows, overgrown shrubbery, and a caving-in roof. Condemned buildings are destined for one outcome—demolition. This is the result the enemy seeks to accomplish in our lives, through condemnation.

Another word for *condemned* is *dammed*. Think about it; when something is dammed up, it is blocked. The flow of something is held back. Other synonyms are *doomed* and *sentenced*. It is as if a person was declared guilty before a trial proved it.

Condemnation brings forth the attitude that says, *I'm not fit to be used by God. What's the point of praying anymore? God isn't going to answer me because I messed up too badly.* It is amazing how many people stop coming to church, or avoid church altogether, because of condemnation. They deem themselves unworthy of even being in the presence of God because of their past mistakes.

The reason condemnation is so discouraging is because it tells us we cannot rise above our shortcomings and slipups. And when we are discouraged, all of a sudden there is that damming affect. The blessing of God is short-circuited because our faith is disrupted. When we feel condemned, we do not have the faith to believe God will bless us. Our lack of faith steals our confidence and robs us of courage and boldness. We feel as if we are not good enough, we don't do enough, and we cannot become everything God wants us to be.

I have found that a lot of people find it difficult to come around Christians because of the judgmental and condemning attitudes so many believers maintain toward others. I have spoken with many who have shared that when they "messed up" in a certain area in their lives, they felt judged and condemned instead of loved and embraced, so they strayed away from church. God does not want us administering condemnation to people who miss the mark, nor does He want us bearing the burden of it in our own lives. There have been times when a church member has seen Taffi and me outside of church and said, "I haven't been to church in a while. But once I get myself together, I'll be back." We can never "get ourselves together" on our own. When we are at our weakest, His strength is made perfect. In our moment of weakness is when we need Him most. Yet for most of us, we run *away* from God instead of *to* Him when we fall.

CONDEMNATION, FEAR, AND GUILT

Our foundations in life are extremely important because they are the platforms upon which our success grows. Psalm 11:3 says if the foundations are destroyed, we are at a serious loss. If we are making decisions based on condemnation and guilt, our base is shaky at best. We are going to have to learn how to be free from condemnation for good. When we miss the mark, we have to know how to handle the sin right away and not allow ourselves to go days, weeks, and even months with a cloud of condemnation hanging over us.

Like every other negative emotion, condemnation is based on fear. One cannot exist without the other. The cycle of condemnation often begins with a bad decision or wrongdoing. We miss the mark or sin, and as a result, we experience negative emotions. We feel bad and start meditating on what we did to such a degree that it invites guilt into our minds. All of a sudden, fear enters our thoughts, and we become afraid of God and those who know Him. We start to feel as if we are alone and that God does not love us as much as He did before we messed up. If left unchecked, these thoughts and feelings will begin to lead us away from the will of God for our lives because we start making decisions based on guilt and condemnation.

I almost lost my life making a decision based on guilt. A good friend of mine really wanted me to minister at a meeting at his church, but I knew in my heart God did not want me to go. I *knew* it was not the will of God for me to minister at that time. But I felt guilty just thinking about turning down the invitation because he was a close friend. Out of allegiance to the friendship, I went ahead and ministered anyway. But while out of town for this meeting I ended up in a terrible car accident that almost took my life. I made a decision out of guilt instead of listening to the voice of God, and the consequences were serious.

We have to look at our own lives and ask ourselves, *What was responsible for this decision I made? Did I make this decision because I was afraid or fearful of something? Did I feel guilty or condemned?* When fear, guilt, and condemnation motivate us, God's Word is no longer the final authority in our lives.

HOW DO WE STOP CONDEMNING OURSELVES?

Knowing the appropriate action to take when we sin and understanding the righteousness of God are critical to avoiding the trap of condemnation. I am convinced people allow themselves to slip into condemnation when they really do not know and understand the love of God or what the blood of Jesus has accomplished on their behalf. It is through His blood that we are able to move beyond the sins of our pasts and remain in a place of peace and confidence. We have the authority to overcome condemnation and allow our emotions to be dominated by the Spirit of God.

So how do we obtain breakthrough where condemnation is concerned?

Realize God Never Condemns You

This was an awesome revelation for me. I came to the realization that even though God never condemns me, sometimes I expect Him to! Traditional religion has affected our thinking to the point where we automatically believe God wants to stamp our lives "Guilty." On the contrary, God is love. He is not *full of* love; He *is* love. Sometimes our minds have problems comprehending the mercy and love of God, especially after we do something that goes against His Word.

John 3:17 says God did not send Jesus into the world to condemn us. He is not the one telling us we are good for nothing and unworthy. Jesus did not use His gifts to go around looking at folks saying, "Yeah, I know what you did last night, and you ought to be ashamed of yourself!" That was not His mission. God sent Jesus into the world so that a condemned world would see there is a way out through Him. He came so that every time feelings of guilt, condemnation, and fear crop up, we can look to Him and say, "Through Jesus, I can get out of this thing. I'm not stuck where I am."

Okay, so you had an abortion, but you are not stuck where you are. Maybe you have gotten a divorce, but you know what? Jesus took condemnation upon Himself so you wouldn't have to.

When the scribes and Pharisees brought the woman caught in adultery to Jesus, He didn't condemn her. Unlike the religious leaders who were quick to judge her, Jesus turned the tables on her accusers and said, "He that is without sin among you, let him first cast a stone." Further, He told the woman He did not condemn her and instructed her to go her way and sin no more (John 8:7–11). The way Jesus handled this situation really shows His heart toward us. He is not quick to cast condemning stones of judgment at people when they miss the mark. Instead, He invites us into His presence where we can receive healing, restoration, and forgiveness.

If You Have Blown It, Confess It

Now, someone may be asking, "Why do I have to confess my sins if God already knows what I've done?" When you confess your sins, shortcomings, and wrongdoing, this is not news to God. This is not for His benefit, but for ours. Through confession, we *get rid of it*. There is something about recognizing our error on our own and confessing it to the Lord. When we do this, that sin is released to Him through our words. He takes the sin and gives us His forgiveness in exchange (1 John 1:9). We are cleansed from our sin and enabled to move forward without fear, guilt, or inferiority.

The whole point of confession is learning to develop the ability to judge ourselves. God expects us to be honest about what we have done that is not pleasing to Him and go humbly before Him, casting everything we are carrying on Him. When we judge what is wrong in our lives, it keeps us in a position of right standing with Him. Confession also arms us against the condemning whispers of the enemy.

Accept God's Mercy, Which Is New Every Morning

The mercy of God must be *accepted*; He is not going to force it on you. Lamentations 3:22 says, "It is because of the Lord's mercy and loving-kindness that we are not consumed, because His [tender] compassions fail not" (AMP). Accepting the mercy of God is a real challenge for a lot of people. We just have a hard time accepting the fact that God loves us! For some reason, it is easier for us to accept the condemnation rather than the love.

Well, you know what? I accept the mercy of God! I choose to reject fear, guilt, and condemnation. It is a decision. There is nothing any of us has done or can do that can stand up against the compassion of God. We may fail, but His compassions do not!

Realize God Is Still Working on You

I fully realize God is still working on Creflo Dollar. This frees me from walking around in condemnation every time I mess up. You have to realize it for yourself also. Philippians 1:6 says, "Being confident of this very thing, that he which hath begun a good work in you will perform it until the day of Jesus Christ." The Lord is not finished with any of us. What we have to grab hold of is this: if He started something in us, He has made a commitment to finish it.

I am convinced that most of us need to have a flashback. We need to flash back to all the good things God has already done for us—when He brought us out of horrible situations and circumstances, turned our lives around, and delivered us from our old lifestyles. Remind yourself of all the times He came through in your finances, just in the nick of time, or when He healed your body. God is so good, and He loves us unconditionally!

I know it's not "religiously" correct to come to God after you have missed the mark, but it is *biblically* correct. It is absolutely in line with His mercy and compassion. He is a loving Father who wants us to turn to Him in our time of need, not retreat into condemnation.

OUR IDENTITY IN CHRIST SETS US FREE

If you have been robbed of your confidence in God, you will not be able to stand when the attacks of the enemy come against you. Condemnation is one of those confidence robbers that always seems to come right before the breakthroughs in our lives. Right at the point where we are about to really get results is where we are attacked. And if we do not know who we are in Christ or lack confidence in the things of God, condemnation will take over.

In Romans 8:1–2, we find the foundation upon which we stand regarding the burden of sin: "There is therefore now no condemnation to them which are in Christ Jesus, who walk not after the flesh, but after the Spirit. For the law of the Spirit of life in Christ Jesus hath made me free from the law of sin and death."

Who are the ones who have no condemnation? Those who have made Jesus Christ the Lord of their lives, those who are *in* Him. We know we are in Him when we do not live our lives according to the dictates of our flesh or our old way of thinking. Condemnation will not be in the life of a person whose thinking lines up with the Word of God. Everything goes back to the way we think. If we accept religious teaching that says God is waiting to strike us with a lightning bolt when we mess up, we are adopting a way of thinking that does not line up with the Word. In doing so, we set ourselves up for condemnation. Love, joy, peace, forgiveness, and compassion are all at the top of God's priority list—not anger, punishment, and destruction.

Verse 2 of Romans 8 gives further insight. There are spiritual laws in effect in the earth, and the two most prominent ones are the law of the Spirit of life in Christ Jesus and the law of sin and death. Condemnation, fear, and guilt are a part of the law of sin and death—the system of operation we all were a part of before coming to know Jesus. But the law of the Spirit of life in Christ Jesus, which is the law of love, is a *higher* law than the law of sin and death. Therefore, if you are operating in the higher law, everything in the inferior law is rendered ineffective in your life. Condemnation cannot control you when you are on Jesus' side!

I don't know about you, but that is good news to me. I don't have to *ever* feel condemned about *anything* when I know who I am in Christ and allow my life to be governed by His law. I just have to make sure I continue to walk in the love of God in order to remain free from the law of sin and death.

As I look at the life of the apostle Paul, I can see how confident he was in his identity in Christ; he was able to declare, "We have wronged no man" (2 Corinthians 7:2). Now this was a man who, before coming to know Jesus Christ, persecuted Christians and had them killed. Imagine the condemnation the enemy attacked him with once he began preaching the Gospel!

In spite of his past, Paul understood what it meant to be redeemed by the love of God. No wonder he operated in such power and saw such strong manifestations in his life and ministry. He was absolutely assured, without a shadow of a doubt, that what God said about him was all that mattered. And the truth of the matter is, our assurance has to be more than just rhetoric. Our actions, speech, and lives must demonstrate our confidence toward God and His love for us.

Listen, when you miss the mark and the devil comes to you and says, "God's not going to hear your prayer because of what you did last night," you need to rebuke that thought because it is an attack against your confidence. If you miss the mark and you ask God to forgive you in the name of Jesus, He hears you. You have to have more confidence in what God has said than you do in how you feel.

We know God is not the one condemning us and making us feel bad about ourselves (Romans 8:34). Our own hearts condemn us when we do not repent of our sins, and Satan has no problem amplifying our faults. Since he is the accuser, it makes sense that he will always try to keep us locked in a prison of condemnation if he can. However, if we miss the mark and ask God to forgive, He is faithful and just to do so (see 1 John 1:9).

BECOMING A PERSON AFTER GOD'S OWN HEART

When we look at the life of David, we can see that God truly does look at our hearts more than at what we did last week. Every sin known to man has already been taken care of by the blood of Jesus. Our righteousness is not determined by our good or bad works; rather, it is determined by what Jesus did for us.

David was described as "a man after God's own heart" (see Acts 13:22). At first I wondered about this because here we have a man who was a murderer and an adulterer, and yet God spoke highly of him. The fact is, even though David missed the mark several times and did some really foolish and selfish things, he loved God and was quick to repent. David was not a man after God's heart because he was sinless, but because he was determined to fulfill the will of God for his life.

God was looking for someone who was going to get the job done, someone who would carry out His plan in the earth, and David was committed to doing that at all costs. The people who fulfill the will of God for their lives are the ones who have hearts just like their Father. He is looking for people who will finish what they have been called to do, even if they have to go through hell and high water to do it. If it takes falling down and getting back up again, as long as they don't quit in the process, they are truly people "after God's heart."

Many have quit on God because of guilt and condemnation. I sometimes look at the empty seats in church services and wonder how many of those spots are empty because people allowed their past or their sin to pull them away from the will of God for their lives. God is looking for soldiers who are willing to stay in active duty long enough to see the fulfillment of His complete plan for their lives. It is one thing to have small victories here and there, but it does not compare with the fullness of what He has in store for each of us if we stay in the game long enough to see the outcome. Everything you may be going through is relevant to your testimony. God can take everything you have ever experienced— the hurt, the pain, the loss, the rejection—and use it all in some capacity.

I often think of the hundreds of times I thought about quitting because of condemnation or other negative emotions that were designed to stop me from reaching my destiny. There have been times I have even allowed condemnation to creep in because of the prosperity in my life. It is during those times that I have to speak to myself and say, *Oh, no, God. Just because there are others who want to live below the standard God has promised doesn't mean I'm going to. God said I would have houses and land. Since God said it, there is no point in my feeling condemned. God promised it to me, and I receive it!*

I had to reject condemnation and recognize I am blessed to be a blessing to others. I am prosperous because I will always have more than enough to do what God has called me to do. I refuse to allow condemnation to enter my thinking and hinder what God has for me.

And yes, you, too, can choose to walk confidently in God's

power and provision, ready to accomplish all that He has called you to do. No matter what you have done in your life, or even what you did last night, remember, condemnation has been defeated by the blood of Jesus. Declare your confidence in the love of God, knowing that if you are loved by Him, there is nothing that can separate you from that love. God loves you with all His being; He loves you as much as He loves Jesus. Because of this love, you are not condemned; instead, you have been set free. You are free to make decisions without fear or guilt. Believe in His love and walk in the liberty of His joy, peace, and confidence that are all rightfully yours.

DEALING WITH ANGER

Anytime anger moves you out of the love of God, it is inappropriate.

⁓ You can feel your heart pounding a mile a minute, adrenaline is rushing through your veins, and you feel your chest tightening. For a moment, you lose all sense of time and space, and your mind starts racing. You feel as if you cannot control the mounting pressure building from deep within. For a brief moment, you contemplate the unthinkable as your mind fills with thoughts of revenge and hostility. You are beyond anger and getting increasingly closer to your breaking point. Sound familiar?

Anger is an emotion with the potential to do a great deal of damage if it is not harnessed and defused. You cannot even begin to imagine the number of crimes that have been committed due to rage left unchecked. When combined with other negative emotions such as inferiority and rejection, anger can turn lethal very quickly, driving people to commit horrendous acts.

Although anger is usually characterized as destructive, there is a type of anger—righteous anger—that compels us to stand for God, and the things of God, in the midst of a world that wants nothing to do with Him. It can move us to allow our light to shine in darkness and stand up for what we know is right. Like fire, anger is neither good nor bad. What matters is how it is used. Learning to differentiate between emotional anger and righteous anger is a key to effective anger management.

What is anger? *Anger* can be defined as an automatic reaction to any real or imagined insult, frustration, or injustice. When I was growing up, if someone spit on you, the natural response was an automatic slap! It wasn't something you thought about; it was an immediate reaction. So, likewise, anger is a reaction. When people are emotionally agitated and do not deal with it in constructive ways, the result will be some sort of aggressive, defensive behavior toward themselves or others. Anger is one of those emotions that *always* seeks expression.

When most of us think about anger, words like *indignation, rage, fury, bitterness, harshness, resentfulness,* and *wrath* readily come to mind. While anger can express itself in these ways, these descriptions are not all-inclusive. We know anger is an emotion. And, like all emotions, it will try to move us in a certain direction.

But here are some questions I want you to consider: Can anger ever move you in a direction of righteousness? Is it always evil? Does God have anything to do with anger? Would He ever condone it? These are very real questions that maybe ten years ago I would have never asked because, in my mind, I automatically concluded any display of anger was wrong.

The Bible has a lot to say about anger, and there are verses in the Word that discuss anger and its potential to be sin. Ephesians 4:31 says, "Let all bitterness, and wrath, and anger, and clamour, and evil speaking, be put away from you, with all malice." Clearly this Scripture tells us to get rid of anger. The apostle Paul also puts anger here in the same category with contention, slander, and having a bad temper—all areas of the flesh.

Psalm 37:8 also says to cease from anger and get away from wrath because they only lead to evil and negative actions. Jesus said, in Matthew 5:22, when we continue to be angry with another person, or harbor malice in our hearts toward him or her, we are in danger of hell's fire! It sounds to me as if God takes anger pretty seriously.

But on the other hand, there are also references to anger that do not sound as harsh. For example, Psalm 4:4 says to be angry, but do not allow that anger to cause you to sin. Ephesians 4:26 says, "Let not the sun go down upon your wrath." The more we look at the Scriptures, the more we begin to see the anger conflict playing out. Clearly, anger is an emotion *we* have the power to control. And, unlike some emotions, it does not always cause a bad result. If this were not the case, God would not instruct us to be mindful of how we handle this powerful emotion.

YOU ARE NOT ALONE

At some point and time, everyone has experienced anger. But how we handle that anger makes all the difference in the circumstances we face in our lives. As we look at Moses and Jesus, we see different accounts where anger was felt and expressed, but with totally different outcomes.

One thing we do not often talk about when looking at the life of Moses is the fact that he had a serious anger problem. We more readily identify him as Israel's fearless leader who parted the Red Sea under the power of God, allowing the Jewish people to escape the Egyptians unharmed. But Moses indeed experienced moments of anger, which compelled him to react based on his emotions.

Exodus 32:19 gives just one example of Moses' angry outbursts: "And it came to pass, as soon as he came nigh unto the camp, that he saw the calf, and the dancing: and Moses' anger waxed hot, and he cast the tables out of his hands, and brake them beneath the mount." When Moses returned from some time spent with God only to find the Israelites having a party and worshiping idols, he became so enraged that he threw the stone tablets containing the Ten Commandments on the mountain, smashing them to pieces. He completely lost control of his emotions.

But this was not the only instance of hot-tempered Moses losing his cool. Moses murdered an Egyptian whom he saw beating a fellow Israelite (Exodus 2:12). And his angry tendencies actually kept him from seeing the promised land, to which he had led his own people:

> And there was no water for the congregation: and they gathered themselves together against Moses and against Aaron. And the people chode with Moses... And the LORD spake unto Moses, saying, Take the rod, and gather thou the assembly together...and speak ye unto the rock before their eyes; and it shall give forth his water, and thou shalt bring forth to them water out of the rock.... And Moses and Aaron gathered the congregation together before the rock, and he said unto them, Hear now, ye rebels; must we fetch you water out of this rock? And Moses lifted up his hand, and with his rod he smote the rock twice: and the water came out abundantly.... And the LORD spake unto Moses and Aaron, Because ye believed me not, to sanctify me in the eyes of the children of Israel, therefore ye shall not bring this congregation into the land which I have given them. (Numbers 20:2–12)

Moses became so frustrated and agitated by the murmuring and complaining of the Israelites that his anger drove him to disobey God's specific instructions, which were to *speak* to the rock so water could flow out of it. God wanted to make sure Moses demonstrated His character before the people, but Moses lost control. He hit the rock out of anger. And while his actions did produce water for the congregation, he was disobedient. God did not want anger to be his motivation. Due to anger, Moses' lack of temperance cost him the right to see the end result of his leadership.

The other type of anger that we see in the Bible is *righteous* anger. The Hebrew word for anger appears approximately 455 times in the Old Testament alone, and out of the 455 anger references, 375 of them refer to the anger of God. We know there is such a thing as righteous anger because we know He is a righteous God.

How can anger be righteous? When we are moved to take a stand to uphold standards and godly character in the midst of disorder or injustice, we exemplify righteous anger. Jesus' anger was based on His love for God and His desire to see God's will accomplished in the Earth.

Mark 3:1–5 documents Jesus' anger with the hypocritical Pharisees. They were constantly trying to find ways to trap Him as they were building their case against Him.

> And he entered again into the synagogue; and there was a man there which had a withered hand. And they watched him, whether he would heal him on the sabbath day; that they might accuse him. And he saith unto the man which had the withered hand, Stand forth. And he saith unto them, Is it lawful to do good on the sabbath days, or to do evil? To save life, or to kill? But they held their peace. And when he had looked round about on them with anger, being grieved for the hardness of their hearts, he saith unto the man, Stretch forth thine hand.

Because of their lack of compassion, Jesus looked at the Pharisees in anger and dismay. They were more concerned with the traditions of their religion than they were with helping people, which was what Jesus came to do. He was angry, and this moved Him to question them and shine a light on their hypocrisy.

In Mark 11, we see another instance where Jesus became angry. Contrary to how Hollywood may portray Jesus, He was not some weak man who had no backbone. Jesus was a man of God, and a man of conviction! He took a stand for what was right, and He stood against what was wrong.

Mark 11:15–17 describes what happened when He entered a synagogue where merchants were selling their goods:

> And they come to Jerusalem: and Jesus went into the temple, and began to cast out them that sold and bought in the

temple, and overthrew the tables of the moneychangers, and the seats of them that sold doves; and would not suffer that any man should carry any vessel through the temple. And he taught, saying unto them, Is it not written, My house shall be called of all nations the house of prayer? But ye have made it a den of thieves.

Jesus turned tables over and physically disrupted what was going on in the synagogue. He was making some things happen! Also, notice in this passage that after Jesus cleaned out the temple, He *taught*. Not only did His anger move Him to action, but it also compelled Him to teach the people why turning the church into a den of thieves was wrong. He used His anger as an opportunity to inspire and enlighten others.

While examining the Scriptures, we see that anger can sometimes cause problems, which was true in Moses' case. Then there are also times when anger is justified, as seen through Jesus' actions. How do we reconcile the two? One is unjustified or emotional anger, and the other is justified or righteous anger.

Justified anger is a sort of detached, righteous indignation. It is what Jesus experienced when He went in the temple. *Unjustified anger* is anger that leads to sin and crimes of passion. For example, when Saul tried to kill David in 1 Samuel 19:10, he was acting out of jealousy, fear, and anger. He was driven by his emotions. This is different from the anger God feels toward unrighteousness.

The Hebrew word most frequently translated "anger" in the Old Testament is the word *aph*. This word is used to describe God's anger in Numbers 11:1: "And when the people complained, it displeased the LORD: and the LORD heard it: and his anger was kindled." The people complained, and it was justifiable for Him to be angry because of their murmuring and complaining, which was sin.

The word for "anger" in the New Testament is the Greek word *orge*. This word refers to the type of anger referenced in Ephesians 4:31. It is also the same Greek word used in Colossians 3:8, which says, "But now ye also put off all these: anger, wrath, malice," and James 1:19, "Wherefore, my beloved brethren, let every man be swift to hear, slow to speak, slow to wrath [*orge*]."

Both the Greek and Hebrew words for anger can actually be used to describe appropriate, questionable, *and* inappropriate anger. Since they can all be used interchangeably, we must look at the context in which anger is being used. This allows us to determine whether the anger is justified or not.

Now, we've already determined that anger, in and of itself, is not good or bad, right or wrong, sinful or holy. Again, I use fire to illustrate this point. By itself, fire is not dangerous or safe; it is neutral. It becomes good or bad based on how it is used. When used for a purpose and within specific boundaries, fire can be beneficial. It can be used for warmth, cooking, and generating power for everyday living.

However, if it is put in the hands of someone irresponsible or sinister, it can cause great destruction. Fire, if allowed to run wild, will destroy everything in its path. We can look at anger in much the same way. It can produce righteous indignation or it can produce emotional sin, depending on how we handle it.

Anytime anger moves you out of the love of God, it is inappropriate. If anger causes us to get into selfishness, manipulation, and self-preservation, we have crossed the line and need to quickly confess those things as sin. James 1:19–20 talks about how the *wrath of man* leads to unrighteousness. This is the anger that tells us to hurt someone else. It is the anger that drives people to murder and exact revenge on those who have hurt or offended them. If our anger does not lead us to act in line with the Word of God, it cannot be justified.

FOUR BIBLICAL PRINCIPLES ABOUT ANGER

Since anger is an emotion that you can exercise control over, realize you do not have to be subject to it. Although we may feel a certain way, this doesn't mean we have to act on it. Consider the following principles:

Control Your Feelings and Never Act on Just Your Feelings

Instead, be compelled to act on the Word of God and emotions that line up with the Word. Whenever negative emotions arise, just remind yourself that emotions were never meant to have authority over you. The way we think determines how we feel, so be sure to fill your mind with the right thoughts. Our feelings should never be the determining factor in the decisions we make. We should first consider what the Word says about the situation, not what our emotions are telling us. If we are angry and tempted to act out on those feelings in a way that could be detrimental to ourselves or others, this is a clear indication that we have been spending time meditating on the wrong things. Change your thoughts by focusing on the Word of God, and your feelings will be transformed to agree with your mind-set.

It is certainly not always easy to overcome anger, and I can speak from personal experience. For years, I really struggled with having a bad temper. My anger would flare up at any time. And many times I took that anger out on my loved ones. Anger drove me to say mean things to people and wound them with those words. The anger was also taking a toll on my body. My blood pressure was skyrocketing and my stress levels were off the charts. I knew if I didn't deal with it quickly, it would eventually destroy my life.

I began to really meditate on the Word and the love of God and allow them to get on the inside and change me. Things began to bother me less and less—to the point where I was no longer quick to fly off the handle every time something did not work out the way I wanted or someone said or did something I didn't like. I began to deal with anger before anger dealt with me.

Don't Be Hasty When Dealing with Anger

Ecclesiastes 7:9 says, "Be not hasty in thy spirit to be angry: for anger resteth in the bosom of fools." In other words, do not be quick-tempered. This verse is describing anger that is out of control. The quick-tempered person is quick to act out. He is easily agitated and doesn't take time to diffuse his anger before acting on it.

Proverbs 15:18 says, "A hot-tempered man stirs up strife, but he who is slow to anger appeases contention" (AMP). Don't be a person who is quick to start a battle out of anger; instead, slow down. Take a moment to clear your head before you say or do anything.

One of my favorite verses, Psalm 103:8, tells us, "The LORD is merciful and gracious, slow to anger, and plenteous in mercy." Can you imagine what would happen if God acted on angry emotions every time one of His children disobeyed Him? I don't think any of us would be here! If God does not become angry quickly as He deals with the whole world, shouldn't we, as His children, strive to be like Him?

Recognize That When You Are Angry, You Are Much More Vulnerable to Sin

Ephesians 4:26–27 says, "'In your anger do not sin': Do not let the sun go down while you are still angry, and do not give the devil a foothold" (NIV). Anger that is maintained, nourished, and nursed becomes an open invitation to the enemy into our lives. Instead of rehearsing the situation, we have to learn to release it. Talk it out, share it with someone who can give you wise counsel, and forgive those who may be involved in the situation. Release the source of your anger by faith, and trust God to assist you in the process.

In Some Cases Anger May Be Righteous, and Its Absence May Displease God

There are times when the absence of anger—being complacent or lukewarm—can actually displease God. Those who are lukewarm usually walk the middle of the road. They do not necessarily agree with the way the world does things, but neither are they on fire for God. A middle-of-the-road person definitely is not going to be passionate about what God is passionate about.

As Christians, we should be people of conviction. We should get angry at sin, the devil, the curse, and everything that is designed to destroy our lives. We should become angry when we see poverty, sin, and sickness attacking our families, when our loved ones are being blinded by the seduction of the world, or when we see so many people who do not know our loving Lord and Savior. We should get upset when we learn of unrighteous laws that are passed, which chip away at the moral fabric of our nation.

Our righteous anger, at the things that oppose our faith and the Word of God, should move us to operate in the authority and power God has given us as His representatives on the earth. We should never allow complacency or deception to cause us to sit idly by and let the enemy run our lives and invade the lives of our loved ones. We must stay on the cutting edge at all times, exercising our authority over *anything* that challenges our position in Christ. Righteous anger, directed at the works of the enemy, will move us to operate in God's power and change what is going on in the world around us.

Even when you are tempted to act on unrighteous anger, try to find a way to turn the tables on it. Instead of allowing anger to drive you to sin, press the pause button and allow it to move you toward righteousness. When people do things to hurt you, instead of cussing them out, bless them and pray for them. Instead of doing something to hurt them, do something kind for them. Upset the plan of the enemy by overcoming evil with good.

Make a decision to walk in love, even if no one else does. Make no mistake, there will always be those who are difficult to love, but you have what it takes to love them by faith. Allow anger to motivate you to speak the truth in love, and watch God back you up every time.

BREAKING FREE FROM REJECTION

Rejection is a negative emotion that begins in the soul.

I am convinced one of the reasons so many people experience emotional turmoil is because one of their most basic human needs—acceptance—has not been met. Every person wants to be accepted and feel important. As the father of three teenage girls, I have come to see this in a different light. Our children need us to accept them for who they are, unconditionally. As children, teenagers, and adults, we all desire to know we are accepted. We all desire to be celebrated and appreciated for who we are. When we feel rejected on some level, it can produce feelings of inferiority, anger, and self-doubt.

The world is full of hurting, rejected people, who really want to be loved unconditionally. The roots of rejection can run deep, causing a host of emotional challenges and behavior that can surface later on in life. Many adults are actually rejected children on the inside, doing everything in their power to gain validation through someone or something outside of God. They seek relationships, jobs, and material things to compensate for what is missing within. The negative emotion of rejection fuels their insecurities and low self-esteem.

Dealing with rejection begins with understanding where it originates and how it gets into our lives. Rejection is a negative emotion that begins in the soul—the realm of the mind, will, and emotions. It starts when a person is actually put down or shunned by someone, and he or she then internalizes the feeling or feelings caused by these actions. When the soul is not healthy, the rest of a person's life will be out of order as well. We've seen that 3 John 2 says it is God's will that we prosper in our souls, which includes having a mind and emotions that are intact and whole. Rejection is a breach in the emotional wholeness God intends for us to experience, and it has the potential to destroy our lives.

We know emotions are feelings on the inside that can take us away from the will of God for our lives. Negative emotions fall under the category of *the flesh*, which does not just refer to the physical body. *The flesh* is a way of thinking that is in opposition to the Word of God. So to walk in the flesh simply means to think, act, and conduct our lives according to a way of thinking that opposes the Word.

Feelings of rejection are what I call "fleshy" because they do not line up with what God says about us or how He looks at us. We are not rejected, but accepted by Him. Receiving and internalizing rejection points to a mind-set that is not in agreement with God.

CLOSE THE ENTRY POINT

Have you ever wondered how the enemy gains access to our lives? He comes in through the avenue of our feelings because, all too often, we continue to fortify and nourish negative emotions. We replay the childhood experiences that scarred us or the situations in life that left us wounded. When we operate in the flesh, it gives Satan the opportunity to come into our lives at any time, through the avenue of the soul.

Rejection hits the very core of a person—that part of ourselves where our sense of value exists, which is why it is such a painful emotion. And when we do not know what God says and thinks about us, we become open to it.

John 6:37 says, "All that the Father giveth me shall come to me;

and him that cometh to me I will in no wise cast out." The Amplified Bible says, "All whom My Father gives (entrusts) to Me will
come to Me; and the one who comes to Me I will most certainly
not cast out [I will never, no never, reject one of them who comes
to Me]." Wow! God's promise is that He will *never* reject a person
who comes to Him.

I start with this Scripture because I want you to know that
despite all who may reject you in your life, there is one upon
whom you can always depend—God. You will always be the apple
of His eye.

Now let's define rejection. Rejection is the feeling of not being
loved or accepted. A person who feels rejected does not feel valuable and usually has extremely low self-esteem. Please hear me;
rejection is a *feeling*, which is exactly why we cannot allow it to
completely take over our lives.

The opportunity to receive rejection is always present, whether
we realize it or not. Often, the decisions we make are determined
by our fear of rejection. For example, men, remember that certain young lady in high school you wanted to ask out on a date?
You picked up the telephone to call or planned how you would
approach her at school, but before you could dial the number or
start up a conversation with her, you got a queasy feeling in the pit
of your stomach. Did you make the phone call or approach her, or
did you let your fear of the word no stop you from even trying?

I remember asking my sisters to fix me up on dates. I wanted
them to ask the girl how she felt about me first so my approach
would be a little bit more confident and my chances of being
rejected would be less. If I felt it was safe, I would walk up to the
girl and ask for her phone number. Now let me tell you, every guy
I knew had a fear of rejection during those crucial moments. Your
mind raced as different scenarios played out in your mind. And as
you waited for the yes or no, the battle with the fear of rejection
raged within you.

And then there was the group of popular kids at school that

you desperately wanted to be a part of. You changed your hairstyle and the way you dressed in order to fit in. And there was the party. You remember—the one where the illegal substance suddenly appeared. You didn't want to lose any "cool" points in the eyes of your peers, so you were faced with a difficult decision. Did you conveniently lower your standards for the sake of remaining in the group, or did you maintain your stance, despite the possibility of rejection? Many of us went with the flow in order to be accepted because we were afraid of rejection.

Rejection issues can come up in other areas as well. Consider a job interview, for example. Some people may embellish their résumés because they really want to make a good impression. Or in the interview, they may become a "yes person" for the interviewer, just to get a couple of brownie points. These people may agree to almost anything if it will lessen their chances of being rejected, only to find out later that they agreed to certain conditions they really were not prepared to carry out.

The potential for rejection is inevitable, which is why we cannot live our lives in fear of it. If you are a salesperson, you are always faced with the possibility that someone will reject your product. In the sports or entertainment arenas, you could be cut from a team or fail to get a contract at any given time. If you are giving a presentation at the office, your supervisor or manager might reject your suggestion and hard work. Even in relationships we risk the possibility of being rejected. The potential for rejection is constant. But learning how to deal with it will enable us to gain the victory over it once and for all.

THREE PITFALLS TO YIELDING TO REJECTION

Rejection, like hurt, is based on fear. And that fear of being rejected is what stops us from moving forward and doing the things we need to do to be successful in a particular area. Fear will always connect us to what we *don't* want to happen, and if our dominant thoughts are fear-based, we will experience the very things we fear, including being rejected.

There are three major reasons why we must eliminate the fear of rejection from our lives. First, when you fear rejection, it causes you to compromise for the sake of conformity. I like to say it like this: compromise is simply changing the question to fit the answer. And even though you change the question to fit the answer, it still does not mean you have the right answer. When facing the fear of rejection, suddenly compromise becomes an option.

When does this compromise occur? It happens whenever your fear of rejection causes you to ignore your values and standards in order to gain acceptance from other people. When you have rejection issues, you will *always* compromise something. Whatever you compromise to keep, you will always end up losing.

Fearing rejection also makes us susceptible to exploitation. In other words, you become willing to do whatever you need to do to be accepted, even if it means turning control of your life over to somebody else. When you are driven by the fear of rejection, you are no longer in the driver's seat. If your main goal in life is to be approved and accepted by other people all the time, you are setting yourself up to be used.

A lot of women who have been hurt but have never healed from past relationships involving rejection fall into the trap of exploitation. It is almost as if they project an energy that attracts men who capitalize on their weakness in this area. When a woman already feels rejected, the need to gain approval in a relationship can easily become all-consuming. She becomes willing to do whatever is necessary to keep a man. This is why women and young girls give something as sacred as their bodies to men whose motives and intentions are wrong. The women feel this is the way to gain the acceptance and love they so desperately seek because they are wounded and rejected.

Even parents who have rejection issues can allow their fears to interfere with good parenting skills. Some fear verbal and emotional rejection from their children to such a degree that they avoid disciplining them properly. They are afraid their children will say, "I don't love you anymore" or become angry with them. So when their children misbehave, they do not spank or reprimand them. A parent's main objective is not supposed to be to become his or her child's best friend. But sometimes it is the fear of being rejected that stops the parent from functioning in his or her role properly.

Whoever you crave acceptance from can ultimately manipulate you because of the power you hand over to him or her. You should never be willing to be accepted at any and all costs. The enemy wants us to become so wrapped up in the fear of rejection that we give ourselves over completely to our emotions rather than surrendering ourselves to God and allowing Him to heal us.

Third, the fear of rejection causes us to lose sight of who we are or abandon our sense of self. People who have a fear of rejection become like chameleons; they change who they are to adapt to whatever situation they find themselves in.

A lot of the chameleons I've encountered are fellow preachers! Many people in the ministry are actually dealing with feelings of rejection, and as a result, they try to adjust who they really are to fit in when around their peers; the way they talk is more "spiritual" around other ministers.

I remember a situation when a man came up to me in public. He had no idea who I was. Something was going on that irritated him, and he just started cussing uncontrollably. After he finished ranting about the situation, he then introduced himself and asked my name and what I did for a living. When I told him who I was and what I did, he immediately said, without skipping a beat, "Praise the Lord, brother!"

FREE AT LAST

Key One: Accept Jesus as Lord and Savior

Because rejection really strikes at the heart of who a person is and has a lot to do with one's self-worth, the first key to becoming free from rejection is to accept Jesus as Lord and Savior of your life. When we become born again, we become new creatures in Christ! Instead of being connected to sin and spiritual death, we are reconnected to the nature of God. We become carriers of all that He is!

As a person with a re-created spirit, you are no longer subject to the curse of being emotionally ruled. This means rejection does not have to ruin your life unless you allow it to. When we accept Jesus as our Savior, we become children of the most high God and joint heirs with Jesus. With Jesus by our side, we do not need to compromise our standards to be accepted by anyone. Not only does God accept us unconditionally, we can trust Him to bring people into our lives with whom we do not feel we have to compromise ourselves and our beliefs.

Key Two: Understand Your Righteousness Through Jesus

The second key to freedom from rejection is our willingness to discover what it truly means to be the righteousness of God. When Adam and Eve disobeyed God in the Garden of Eden, they exposed all of mankind to the curse from that point on. Instead of fellowship and communion with God, they invited the curse upon the earth, which included sin, disease, poverty, and physical and spiritual death—ultimately, separation from Him. Every negative emotion became a part of their consciousness. In fact, immediately after they sinned, they discovered they were naked and began to feel rejected rather than accepted by the Father. As a result, they hid in the midst of the garden, as they no longer felt worthy in God's eyes. Every human being who would ever be born would now be born into sin, through no choice of his or her own.

God sent Jesus to the earth to redeem mankind from the curse of sin. Through Him, we are all able to come into relationship with God once again and remain in fellowship with Him forever. When Jesus sacrificed Himself on the cross, He did not just take on sin, He *became* sin, so a divine exchange could take place—our sin in exchange for His righteousness. Jesus not only died physically, He also died spiritually, and experienced separation from God. When He defeated the enemy in hell and was resurrected, the job was done. We now have the right to be called children of God!

So righteousness is not something any of us can earn. No amount of good works could ever qualify us to become righteous in God's eyes, just as there was nothing we had to do to qualify as sinners other than to be born! Righteousness is a free gift you can receive through Jesus.

Developing a righteousness-consciousness really helps to get rid of rejection. When you *know* you have been made righteous, you have confidence you have been accepted by God. There is no sense of guilt, condemnation, or rejection. There are only love, peace, and joy that come from knowing you have a special place in God's heart. There is nothing you can do to cause Him to turn His back on you.

Think about how good it feels to be accepted for who you are, without judgment or criticism. This is how God sees us! There is no room for rejection in the heart of a believer who knows who he or she is in Christ.

Key Three: Forgive

Forgiveness is a vital part of getting rejection out of our lives. When we are rejected by someone, the rejection can lead to anger, resentment, bitterness, and strife. And when we hold on to these negative emotions, refusing to forgive those who have rejected us, we give them power in our lives.

All unforgiveness does is hurt *you* in the long run. Instead of spending energy holding on to what others did to you, just forgive them and remind yourself, *Boy, they just don't know what they're missing. I'm awesome!*

Sometimes all it takes is reminding ourselves of all the great qualities we possess to change our perspective. A slight shift in how we look at the situation can push us in the right direction emotionally. Sometimes we just allow too much drama to come into our lives. We become willing victims of our own issues rather than progressive overcomers in Christ. You cannot control what other people think or say about you, so stop worrying about it! Forgive them for what they have done to you and move on.

Key Four: Become Aware of Others' Pain

It is amazing what happens when you choose to become aware of the pain of others rather than focus on your own, which is why the fourth key to ridding your life of rejection is so important. Recognize that someone else has been hurt more than you. Something special happens in your life when you seek to help others who have gone through worse things than you have. Hearing their stories can even provide an opportunity for you to minister to them, allowing you to heal in the process. When you become so busy extending love toward someone else who is in emotional turmoil, you take your focus off yourself, which is what the love of God is all about.

Key Five: Stop Being Codependent

Finally, break free from codependency on people. Recognize you can love and admire people, but never allow people to determine how you feel and carry yourself. A great way to become more comfortable with yourself is to take time to do things and go places by yourself. There is nothing wrong with treating yourself to a nice dinner or a movie. In fact, it can be a great way to learn how to stop depending on others for happiness and approval. When you can get to the place where you enjoy spending time with yourself, self-esteem increases, and the chains of rejection are broken.

LET GO OF THE PAST

I have known and counseled people who chose to hold on to the hurt and pain of past rejection. This behavior is usually common among those who had an absent parent. Growing up in a situation where you feel rejected by one or both parents is tough, especially if you never had the opportunity to know them. A child grows up with unanswered questions that can develop into rejection, deeply rooted from within.

However, even if you did have a parent who abandoned or fell short of his or her parental responsibilities, you have someone even greater! God can and will fill the void in your heart. We must refuse to remain stuck in hurt and past rejection and let go of the past if we are ever to move forward.

Letting go is not easy, and you may not even know *how* to let go. You can start with the words you speak. Begin making declarations every day that reflect where you want to go emotionally. If you are dealing with rejection, begin to declare you are not rejected but accepted by God. You are His beloved, and nothing can separate you from His love. Speak where you want to go rather than rehearsing the problem. As your words start to change, you will find your thoughts and emotions beginning to change as well. Instead of feeling rejected, you will begin to realize the love of God surrounding you every day.

Since the words you speak and internalize will determine your thought life and ultimately your emotions, daily meditation on the Word of God is an important key to overcoming rejection. Meditate on the promises of God concerning His love and faithfulness toward you to renew your mind in this area. Allow the image He has of you to become imprinted on your soul.

The truth is, being accepted by others, while comforting, should not be a lifetime goal. God has already given you the standard upon which to base your feelings—His Word. Line your feelings up with that standard, and you will notice a difference in your emotions.

We have all experienced rejection at some point in our lives. But as overcomers, we have to stand up and fight against it by reminding ourselves who we are in Christ. He always causes us to triumph in every emotional battle we face. The advantage we have as Christians is that we have God in our lives. We have a God who has accepted us and committed to never reject us. And that relationship empowers us to live a life free of rejection.

DON'T STRESS OUT!

We do not have to be troubled by stressful situations—
because we believe and trust in God.

Did you know stress is a silent killer that destroys lives, disrupts marriages, and wreaks havoc on our health? Stress and anxiety are estimated to affect well over 19 million people in the United States alone, and that number is growing daily. Hypertension, strokes, and heart attacks are just a few of the negative consequences of stress.[1] With so many people dealing with pressure on their jobs and concerns about the future, it is not surprising that stress is at an all-time high. When crisis comes, most people do not know how to handle it. As a result, they become stressed-out and burned out, with no apparent *way* out.

One way to look at stress is from the standpoint of how a building is constructed. The word *stress* can be used to describe the pressure placed on certain structures in relation to their ability to provide support. Unfortunately, stress has become a destructive term rather than a constructive one because it is destroying so many lives.

Everyone has the ability to deal with stress, but not everyone knows exactly how to. We can be sure that we will encounter situations in life that have the *potential* to disrupt our peace and tempt us to give in to our emotions. But we have to learn what to do when faced with potentially stressful situations.

I want to revisit the construction illustration to show the

connection between stress and our ability to handle it. Any building is equipped to handle a certain amount of weight. In fact, it is built with certain specifications in mind for this very purpose. However, when more pressure is placed on that structure than was originally intended, problems arise.

So, likewise, when we take on stress we were never created to bear, we end up carrying more than God ever intended. Eventually, we crumble under the weight of life's circumstances. So it is important that we become what the Bible calls *prudent*. A person who is prudent knows how to manage his or her life in such a way that balance is maintained at all times.

IDENTIFY THE PROBLEM

Proverbs 1:17 says, "Surely in vain the net is spread in the sight of any bird." You may be wondering what such a Scripture has to do with stress. I want you to think about it. If a net were spread in front of a bird, it would fly around, above, or away from it. Because the bird identifies the net as a hindrance to its ability to move freely, the net becomes an enemy to it.

Similarly, we must view stress as an enemy to our happiness and health, or we will not avoid it when potential stressors show up in our lives. Stress is not something you should accept as okay without realizing that it is designed to steal your joy. The wise person, like the instinctive bird, sees the trap laid out before him and avoids it.

How do we know when we are dealing with stress? Many times the presence of the following is an indication:

- Forgetfulness
- Bad temper
- Chronic fatigue

- Cynicism

- A sense of helplessness

- Never having a sense of accomplishment

- Feeling like a failure

- Constant illness

- Headaches, tension, high blood pressure, heart disease

After reading this list, which is by no means exhaustive, we can see that tolerating stress can prove to be both dangerous and costly to our health and our lives. Some studies suggest that life-threatening diseases such as cancer have even been tied to stress.[2] If you are experiencing any of these warning symptoms, I am fairly certain there is a connection between your stress levels and how you feel physically, emotionally, and mentally.

If the root to a particular problem is not dealt with, the fruit will continue to grow. This is also the case with stress. Many times, people deal with their physical ailments from the stand-point of treating the symptoms rather than eliminating what is causing the problem. The aforementioned list can be compared to the fruit of a tree. These are the "fruit" issues that manifest in a person's life, which grow from a root of stress. Pay attention to what is going on in your body, as well as your mind, because signs and symptoms of physical distress could very well be indicators of unchecked stress.

LEARNING HOW TO DEAL

Identifying stress in your life is the first step, but the next question is: how do you deal with it properly? The Word of God always provides the answers we need to life's toughest questions. Second

Corinthians 4:8 describes the troubles we face in life: "We are hedged in (pressed) on every side [troubled and oppressed in every way], but not cramped or crushed; we suffer embarrassments and are perplexed and unable to find a way out, but not driven to despair" (AMP).

The truth is, we will all have trouble at times. But just because we have trouble doesn't mean we have to be stressed out by it. It is how we handle the situations that makes the difference.

Years ago, I wrote a book titled *How to Trouble Your Trouble*. In it I discussed the importance of making sure we take the right stance in the midst of challenges. Stress comes from the outside in, through pressure and various circumstances over which we may or may not have control. The key is to make sure we are ready for what comes our way at any given time. We can prepare by building ourselves up on God's Word and keeping what *He* says at the forefront of our minds at all times. Know how to respond to the trouble *before* it comes.

John 14:1 gives us the formula for dealing with stress. It is our first line of defense: "Do not let your hearts be troubled (distressed, agitated). You believe in and adhere to and trust in and rely on God; believe in and adhere to and trust in and rely also on Me" (AMP). Jesus said the best way to handle the pressure is to *make a decision to not be affected by it!* Your attitude when you are going into a battle determines the outcome. If you always maintain a mind-set that says, *You know what? I am not going to let* anything *rob me of my peace and joy,* you set up a mental barrier that keeps the effects of stress out of your life.

The second part of this Scripture discusses *why* we do not have to be troubled by stressful situations—because we believe and trust in God. When we know God is more than able to bear our burdens and orchestrate the circumstances in our lives, it really relieves us of the pressure.

Understanding that we need to put our trust in God in order to shut out stress means we have a part to play. It requires spending time with God through His Word and prayer and learning how to hear from Him. The more time you spend meditating on His promises, getting them in your heart and allowing them to affect your thinking, the more you will begin to hear Him speak words of encouragement to you—words specifically tailored for your situation. It is the spoken word we hear within, as we study and meditate on the written Word, that further strengthens our faith and reinforces our trust in God's ability to fight our battles.

Jesus explained in Matthew 24:6 that we have no reason to be stressed. "And ye shall hear of wars and rumors of wars: [pay close attention to what He says next] see that ye be not troubled." We have a very present help in the times of trouble, and He delivers us out of them all (see Psalm 34:19).

What would happen to your stress level if you meditated on the truth that God will always deliver you out of trouble? How differently would you feel if you were to immediately say, "The Lord will deliver me from this"? It is when we meditate on the problem that we begin to allow stress to overpower our lives. Instead, we must allow God's Word to consume our thinking. We've got to start declaring, "I know trouble is here, but things are going to work out in my favor. I always win, for God is my helper! I don't know how He will do it, but I trust God" (see Psalm 54:4). These are the types of confessions that stress-proof our lives.

WHAT'S THE CAUSE?

Figuring out what is causing stress in our lives is one of the most important things we can do to eliminate it. Once we discover the reasons why we feel the way we do, we can locate God's Word on the matter so we can combat those issues. Let's look at some of the reasons we become stressed-out.

Uncertainty

When we are not sure about how things will work out, we can really become stressed-out. However, we can control the harvest we receive in life. Our future does not have to be uncertain. Because of the law of seedtime and harvest, what we sow is what we reap; therefore, our future is in our seed. For example, we do not have to wonder if God will bless us because, as we bless others, we will be blessed. Likewise, as we forgive others, we will be forgiven. This is a truth you can count on. Whatever we sow, we will reap.

The law of sowing should clear up the issue of uncertainty for anyone dealing with it. Just as a farmer plants seed in the ground and expects a crop from that seed, we can also expect to receive what we give. The Word gives absolute certainty about how things are going to turn out in our lives.

If uncertainty is one of the reasons you are stressed-out, you can eliminate that by reminding yourself what Jesus said in John 14:1: "Ye believe in God, believe also in me." Believe in the Word of God because in it there is absolute certainty. And if you are not certain of it, you need to meditate on it until it becomes more real to you than the situations or circumstances that are causing stress in your life.

Having assurance delivers us from stress. It is that sense of knowing that you know. I made a decision that I am not going to waste my time and energy being stressed-out. After we finished building the World Dome I said, "Well, praise God; that's it!" Now we are tackling other projects that are even bigger! I have decided to refuse to stress about finances and resources. I trust God 100 percent.

Unresolved Conflict

Unresolved conflict will also cause stress. The Word instructs us to be at peace with all men (see Romans 12:18). Negative emotions toward others such as bitterness, unforgiveness, and selfish anger will poison your soul and disrupt your relationship with God. The only one being hurt by these feelings is you.

Forgiving people does not mean you are saying what they did to you is okay. What it says is that you acknowledge it was wrong, but you are willing to let it go, out of obedience to God. Forgiveness is not an option; it is a requirement from God. When bitterness, hurt, and unresolved issues toward others begin to build up in our hearts, it starts affecting us spiritually, emotionally, and physically.

Many people have walked away from our ministry because of offense. Too often we have wrong motives and petty reasons for why we do things. It is time for us to grow up and out of bitterness rather than allowing stressors such as negative emotions toward others to disturb our lives. Instead of running away from our inner conflicts, we must admit them and face them head-on. If you have bitterness and unforgiveness against anyone, let it go.

Unrealistic Comparisons

Comparing ourselves to others is a huge stressor. King Saul was a perfect example of what can happen when we begin to compare our gifts and abilities with someone else's. When the women began to sing, "Saul hath slain his thousands, and David his ten thousands," Saul took his eyes off the victories he had been blessed with and immediately started to compare himself with David (1 Samuel 18:7–11). And that is where his stress began. As a result of comparing himself to David, Saul became jealous and angry. His negative emotions moved him to even try to kill David.

I see this happen frequently in ministry. One preacher compares his ministry with another preacher's ministry. This is not wise because God has called different people to do things in different ways. If you have a five-hundred-seat church, but you begin to compare yourself to the guy who has a ten-thousand-seat church, you belittle the miracle God did for you to get that five-hundred-seat church.

Second Corinthians 10:12 says, "For we dare not make ourselves of the number, or compare ourselves with some that commend themselves: but they measuring themselves by themselves, and comparing themselves among themselves, are not wise." When you compare, you belittle. Belittle what? You belittle what God has done for you and in you. You start comparing your car with somebody else's new car, or you compare your clothes or physical appearance to someone else's. Comparison breeds competitive jealousy and ungratefulness. It keeps stress levels high as we struggle to find ways to obtain and maintain unnecessary things to compete with others. It is just not worth it.

Unconfessed Sins Will Cause Stress

I often say, when we confess our sins, this is not news to God. He knows our hearts and everything we do. We stress ourselves out when we carry the burden of sin and do not take advantage of the provisions God has made available to us through the blood of Jesus.

We've seen that 1 John 1:9 says, "If we confess our sins, he is faithful and just to forgive us our sins, and to cleanse us from all unrighteousness." What a relief to know that if we admit our wrongdoing to God, He will forgive us unconditionally!

It is harmful and even dangerous for us as Christians to know we have sin in our lives but not admit it. When we refuse to acknowledge our sins, self-deception creeps in, and we begin to believe sin is really okay.

A great way to make sure you get sin out of your life is to judge yourself on a daily basis. I like to take time at the end of every day to examine what I did and said that day as I talk with God. The Word says if we judge ourselves, we won't be judged (Matthew 7:1). But if we deceive ourselves and refuse to confess our sins to

God, judgment is knocking at our door. Take time daily to look at your life and say, "You know what? That was wrong. I shouldn't have said that. Lord, please forgive me." Deal with sin in your life so that it doesn't show up in the form of stress.

Unusual Pressure in the Area of Finances

Financial pressure is a common stressor in the lives of people from all walks of life. Many times the pressure comes from a lack of discipline where spending is concerned. Some simple adjustments in money management can usually eliminate a majority of stress relating to finances. Simply put, stop spending more than you earn.

There are so many people who are trapped in bad financial situations that they have created for themselves. Are you engaged in hyperconsumption? Is your outgo exceeding your income? Are you buying things you cannot afford? For example, you should not consider buying a $200,000 house if you only make $25,000 a year! I know people who actually did things like this, and I saw their lives crumble around them due to the pressure of trying to maintain a lifestyle they simply could not afford.

Eliminating unnecessary financial pressure will really get rid of stress, so take a moment to locate yourself in this area. True prosperity does not involve being stressed-out from the beautiful house and car we cannot afford. When God blesses us, there is no sorrow attached. Meditate on the Word of God more than you do acquiring material items. Focus on being a giver and supporter of those in need. When we sow these types of seeds, we are guaranteed to see what we give come back to us in a greater measure.

If pressure from financial situations is stressing you out, it may also be the result of a lack of order in your life. Don't use prosperity as an excuse to be unorganized and sloppy in the way you handle your affairs. When your life, marriage, household, or finances are out of order, a certain amount of stress will be present. Have a plan for your life and finances.

FIVE PRACTICAL KEYS TO STRESS RELIEF

I am a firm believer in the value of practicality, which is why these five keys to stress relief are so important. I encourage you to implement them as part of your action plan for ridding your life of stress for good.

Key One: Write Things Down

I used to think it was necessary and important that I be able to recall things without writing them down. Then I realized it was causing me unnecessary stress. I was trying to remember things I needed to do, people I needed to call, and dates and appointments I needed to keep, and it was becoming burdensome. Don't try to conduct your life this way. Write things down.

Key Two: Stop Trying to Please Everybody

You cannot please everyone. At one point, I took on the attitude that I was going to be a pastor who pleased everybody; however, I quickly learned this was impossible. Instead of pleasing people, I ended up wanting to fight some of them! Stop stressing out trying to be everything to everyone. Instead, focus on pleasing God by obeying His Word and being the best person you can be.

Key Three: Take Care of Your Body

You will be amazed at how good you feel and how stress melts away when you do simple things like exercise regularly, eat food that nourishes your body, and get proper rest. Not only do these things help you recover from stressful situations throughout the day, but they also help your body handle stress more efficiently.

We were created to be active, which is why exercise should be a part of life. It is a great stress reliever, and it can help protect against high blood pressure, muscle loss, and obesity. With a strong heart and healthy body, you will feel more equipped to take on the challenges of day-to-day life.

Key Four: Stop Jump-Starting Your Body with False Energy

Consuming a lot of caffeine or sugar may give you a quick burst of energy, but it also makes you feel as if you can handle more than you really can. You may take on more than you are able to and end up "crashing" at the end of the day because of the effects of caffeine or sugar on the body.

Key Five: Talk to Your Problems Rather than About Them

You have the potential to drastically affect your stress levels by deciding what you give your attention to. Many times we rehearse our problems to ourselves and with others. This only magnifies and amplifies what we are dealing with. The Word says we are to speak to our mountains in faith (not about them), and they will be removed (Mark 11:23–24).

God's solution to stress is very clear. Philippians 4:8 instructs us to keep our minds focused on only positive things. Our emotional health is just as important as our physical health, and it is affected by what we think and speak about on a regular basis. Our words direct our thought patterns, so we must choose to speak only the outcome we want to see. Your body will respond to negative thoughts just as if the actual events are taking place, so guard against unwanted stress by casting down negative thoughts and speaking the Word of God.

Let's make a decision today to receive the peace of God. Cast the cares of life on Him by verbally declaring what He has said rather than rehearsing your problems. Take responsibility for your emotional and physical health by making lifestyle choices that alleviate stress and increase vitality in every area. Don't stress out, and most importantly—trust God!

FEAR: PUBLIC ENEMY #1

Fear is dangerous because it connects us to the things
we fear.

Have you ever heard someone say having a little fear is
natural, or that fear can help push you to accomplish your goals?
Let me be absolutely clear: fear is not natural, nor is there anything positive to be gained from it. In fact, allowing fear to take up
residence in your mind and heart can actually be more dangerous
than you realize. The world's crises and concerns are all based on
fear. And with so many people receiving the fear that is pumped
through the media outlets, it is no wonder we are seeing an explo-
sion of negative things taking place all around us. Though the
temptation to fear seems overwhelming at times, we must resist
it. Fear is public enemy number one, a spiritual force designed to
connect us to the very things we *do not* want to happen. Because of
this, it is vital we do not give fear *any* place in our lives.

During the sudden outbreak of a virus called H1N1, otherwise
known as the swine flu, I remember the media frenzy that contributed to the global panic that began to take place as people
started expecting this virus to hit the global scene. Sure enough,
it hit and began to claim lives. It seemed everywhere you turned
the swine flu was talked about. The truth is, news reports began
feeding the general public's fear before anything even happened.
Soon there were pictures of people wearing surgical masks. People
were afraid to ride airplanes or even visit public places with large

crowds. It seemed the more the news media talked about it, the more fearful people became. It was not long before we began to hear about children and adults dying of the disease.

As I thought about the whole swine flu issue, I began to consider how fear is contagious, and words have the potential to spread like a deadly cancer, affecting the thinking of large groups of people. Once fear is accepted and internalized, it has the power to bring to pass the very things we fear. The swine flu is just one example of this spiritual law.

Contrary to the many suggestions the enemy brings to us, living a fearless life is attainable. When you are connected to God through Jesus, there is an empowerment available to conquer any situation. Being a conqueror simply means you win *every* battle all the time. This person does not overcome every now and then. He consistently has victory in every area of his life, including victory over fear.

WHAT IS FEAR?

Fear is a spiritual force. I have often described it as being the reciprocal or opposite of faith. Faith and fear are directly opposed to each other. Faith connects you with the promises of God, and fear connects you with the negative outcomes. It is actually *faith in the negative.*

The spirit of fear first entered the earth through sin in the Garden of Eden. Life for Adam and Eve before the fall can be likened to a power cord plugged into a socket. Their spirits were plugged into God, who was their source of life, love, and power. As a result of their being connected to Him, they had access to everything in Him, and His power flowed through them. They only knew and experienced the benefits of being attached to God.

However, something devastating happened when they ate of the fruit of the Tree of the Knowledge of Good and Evil. All of a sudden, they were disconnected from the Spirit of love, who is

God, and became connected to the spirit of fear, who is Satan. As a result, they immediately were thrust into a life of self-preservation. This same spirit of fear is what governs the lives of people who do not know God, as well as those who know Him but allow fearful thoughts to infiltrate their minds. Once fear is received, it can work its way down into our spirits and begin affecting our words and actions.

There are those who think fear is just a natural part of life, that there is nothing we can do about it. But natural things come from God, and the Word tells us God does not give us the spirit of fear. Satan *is* the spirit of fear because he is the tormenter.

First John 4:18 says, "There is no fear in love; but perfect love casteth out fear: because fear hath torment. He that feareth is not made perfect in love." Fear and torment are attached to one another, which is why anytime you are in fear, nagging thoughts, paranoia, and a lack of peace regarding whatever you are concerned about gnaw at you on a constant basis.

God cannot be connected to tormenting, fearful thoughts. What He *does* give us is love, power, discipline, and a sound mind (2 Timothy 1:7). God is love, and love is the power that fuels the kingdom of God. Believers have spiritual forces at work inside of them at all times—love, joy, peace, long-suffering, gentleness, and so on. Our spirits are constantly producing these things, not fear. If fear gets a foothold in our lives, it is because we allowed it to come in from the outside.

Just as you cannot have faith without the Word of God, you cannot have fear without the words of Satan. And these words are swirling around us all the time. The enemy cannot do anything without first speaking words to our minds. And anything he speaks is infused with fear.

Consider the times in your life when you were tormented with fear. Your thinking may not have been sound, and you may have even been irrational. That is what fear does to us. It causes us to panic! There was a time when my wife, Taffi, struggled with the spirit of fear. Because of fear, she would turn all the lights on in the house if she was home alone. And to make matters worse, we used to pull pranks on each other by jumping out of the closet unexpectedly! I realized what we were considering harmless fun was actually helping to support the spirit of fear she had, and it was planting seeds of fear in me as well.

We must also pay attention to the words we speak that are based in fear. "That scared me to death" and "I'm afraid I won't be able to make it tonight" are common phrases used in everyday conversation. They are also laced with fear. When these types of things are spoken, even in casual discussion, they activate the wrong spiritual laws.

Proverbs 4:23 says, "Keep thy heart with all diligence; for out of it are the issues of life." Since fear works its way into our hearts from the outside, it is our responsibility to keep it out. The gates to the heart are the eyes, ears, and mouth, so we must make sure we are not giving our attention to fearful words and images. For example, watching the eleven o'clock news every night is not going to help you keep fear out of your mind. Instead, it will prove to plant and nourish seeds of fear. If you continually look at and listen to all the bad reports about murder, death, crime, and disasters taking place throughout the world, you give the devil something to work with. And it won't be long before you find yourself up at night with all the lights turned on.

WHY FEAR IS SO DANGEROUS

God commands us not to fear throughout the Bible, from Genesis to Revelation. Fear is not okay because it actually gives the enemy direct access to *everything* concerning us. It enables him to make our lives his playground.

The account of Job is a perfect example of how fear can devastate a person's life. If you are not familiar with the story, Job was an extremely wealthy man, who lived a life full of integrity and honorable character before God. He had divine favor and protection from the Lord (Job 1:10). However, Job's problem was that he continually offered sacrifices on behalf of his children (Job 1:5). He felt he needed to offer the sacrifices on their behalf to ensure their protection.

Does this sound familiar? As parents, how many times have we prayed for our children based on the fear that if we didn't, something bad might happen to them? Job's sacrifices for his children were based in fear, not faith, and his actions actually opened the door for the enemy to access his possessions and family.

In Job 3:25, he says, "For the thing which I greatly feared is come upon me, and that which I was afraid of is come unto me." Job's fear-based, religious rituals did nothing more than bring destruction to his household. This is why fear is so dangerous; it actually connects us to the things we fear.

This situation was one example of how fear connects us to what we do not want, but it also works in other areas as well. The fear of death, if not dealt with, will lead to death. The fear of failure will connect us to failure. If you have a nagging fear of dying young or developing some fatal disease, believe me, it is only a matter of time before it becomes a reality. Fear is just that powerful.

The very connective nature of fear is the reason Jesus was constantly instructing people not to fear. He knew something they didn't—that fear would contaminate their faith and stop the power of God from moving.

There were critical moments in Jesus' ministry where a healing or deliverance was on the line, and He let people know they had to get rid of fear. Luke 8:49–50 says, "While he yet spake, there cometh one from the ruler of the synagogue's house, saying to him, Thy daughter is dead; trouble not the Master. But when Jesus heard it, he answered him, saying, Fear not: believe only, and she shall be made whole." Jesus instructed them not to fear because it would cancel the faith that was necessary for this miracle to take place.

I've heard people say, "A little fear is good for you." And I used to think the same thing. However, fear is not good for anyone, in any way. People do not realize God puts fear in the same category as a host of other sins. Revelation 21:8 says, "But the fearful, and unbelieving, and the abominable, and murderers, and whoremongers, and sorcerers, and idolaters, and all liars, shall have their part in the lake which burneth with fire and brimstone: which is the second death." Notice that the first two categories of people who will inherit hell are the fearful and the unbelieving.

The pairing of these two sins lets us know we cannot be in fear without being in unbelief. When we fear, we are essentially saying we do not believe God can take care of us, protect us, and provide for us. It is having faith in the wrong things, and the Bible calls an unbelieving heart evil (Hebrews 3:12).

Fear is a thief that tries to steal our confidence in God and His Word. As believers, we *believe*! And yet God says we are *not* believing Him if we have fear on any level. Fear will always try to rob us of our status as believers.

For those who hold to the false belief that a little fear won't hurt you, I suggest really taking the time to look at what Revelation 21:8 says, and put fear in the same category as all the other sins mentioned in that passage. The "just a little fear" argument does not add up.

If a little fear is okay, then what about a little lying, a little adultery, and a little murder? If a little fear is okay, then a little whoremongering must be acceptable in God's eyes, too, right? Wrong! Fear is a sin just like any other, and it should never be tolerated.

MIND-SETS TO CONQUER FEAR

The overcomer's mind-set is one that is fearless and conscious of God's presence at all times. When you know God is with you, and that He will never leave or forsake you, fear disappears. The fearless mind-set is a conqueror's mind-set that is confident in victory, no matter what we are facing. We are certain of God's ability to handle the situation on our behalf. In addition, there are some specific attitude adjustments we must make to eradicate fear.

We Must Know and Believe the Love God Has for Us

This is the most important step to overcoming fear. When you do not believe God loves you, you are open to deception from the enemy. Condemnation, guilt, and a sense of unworthiness are all designed to get us to doubt God's love for us. Knowing what the Bible says is critical to combating these negative emotions.

First John 4:16 says, "And we have known and believed the love that God hath to us. God is love; and he that dwelleth in love dwelleth in God, and God in him." Now that is a powerful verse. We have to settle in our hearts that God does not just have love, He *is* love. God loves us, and we are a permanent part of His heart because of that love. He always has us on His mind, and we are always in His heart! Being armed with this kind of knowledge and fully persuaded by it make it difficult for the enemy to convince us otherwise.

The more we think about and internalize the revelation of God's love for us, the more we develop confidence in His ability to take care of us in *every* area of our lives. Believing God can and *will* take care of all our needs—financially, emotionally, physically, and spiritually—eliminates fear (1 John 4:18). Love is fear's antidote.

Recognize most fear comes from not knowing what the future holds.

People who do not intimately know God through a personal relationship are ruled by and subject to fear. This is because they have no idea what their future really holds; they have no hope.

Ephesians 2:12 describes the spiritual condition of the person who is not in relationship with Jesus Christ:

[Remember] that you were at that time separated (living apart) from Christ [excluded from all part in Him], utterly estranged and outlawed from the rights of Israel as a nation, and strangers with no share in the sacred compacts of the [Messianic] promise [with no knowledge of or right in God's agreements, His covenants]. And you had no hope (no promise); you were in the world without God. (AMP)

I cannot imagine what it would be like to be in the world right now without God. When you are separated from God, you are separated from all the wonderful benefits of His covenant, which includes the hope and promise of a glorious, successful, and prosperous future, not just in heaven, but on the earth as well. While you are here, God desires you to live life to the fullest.

God has a wonderful plan for those who are a part of His kingdom. We have so much to look forward to! But when you have no hope, the only things you can do are worry and fear what the future holds.

John 16:13 gives yet another reason we do not have to fear the future when we know God: it says the Holy Spirit will *show us things to come*! Darkness brings fear, but when light shines in the midst of darkness, fear flees the scene. The inside information the Holy Spirit will give you is like the light switch that is turned on in a dark room. Once you can see where you are going, there is no reason to fear!

To me, it is absolutely thrilling to know I can have complete knowledge of what my future holds. I may not know exactly how God is going to get me there, but I do know my outcome is going to be a favorable one.

Recognize Fear Comes from Feeling Powerless About the Future

A feeling of powerlessness is one of the main reasons people act out on fear-based, negative emotions. How do you fix this? By recognizing your future is in your seed. So, as we sow the seed of God's Word in our hearts, we know exactly what we are going to harvest.

See, the only people with uncertain futures are those who do not plant the seed of the Word in their hearts. Everything in the earth operates according to a fail-proof system called seedtime and harvest (Genesis 8:22). This is a spiritual law that always yields results—positive or negative. When the right seeds are sown, you can always expect your future to be successful.

Even in the financial realm, the seedtime and harvest system is constantly working. Principles such as "Give and it shall be given to you" are available for anyone who will get involved. If you want to secure your financial future, there is a way—be a giver! The same is true for any other area of your life. You have more power than you realize.

Your future is wrapped up in your seed. Let me give you a practical example. If you go to the store and buy a pack of seeds, you will see a picture on the pack that shows you what the final product is going to look like. You already know what is going to happen when you put that seed in the ground and nurture it.

Likewise, your future is wrapped up in the Word of God. It is the picture that foretells what your end will be if you follow its instructions. God is essentially saying, "Take My Word and put it in your heart by meditating on it day and night. Read it, listen to it, and talk about it. Act on it and allow it to become a part of you. If you plant it deep within the soil of your heart, it will grow a wonderful future for you."

A person who does not know his future is allowing some other kind of seed other than the Word of God to get in his heart. Jesus painted a clear picture of what would happen to people in the last days in Luke 21:26: "Men swooning away or expiring with fear and dread and apprehension and expectation of the things that are coming on the world; for the [very] powers of the heavens will be shaken and caused to totter" (AMP).

I used to think this Scripture was specifically referring to people dropping dead because of heart attacks brought on by fear, and I believe that is part of it. But the Lord spoke to me about this passage and said, "Son, that's not the only thing I'm talking about here. Men's hearts will fail them because of fear. Out of a man's heart are the issues of life, and the soil of a man's heart won't produce a harvest because fear is there." But when we put God's Word in our hearts and guard against fear, we will see results. We are not powerless over our futures.

I cannot tell you what is going to happen with everyone else in the world, but I can tell you what is going to happen for those who know the love of God and execute the law of seedtime and harvest. We are going to see the harvest due to us.

We Must Live by Faith

Faith is the lifestyle of the Christian. It is not an option! We are to *live* by faith, meaning we do not live by our physical senses—what we can see, taste, touch, feel, and smell, but we live by the Word of God. Living by faith means making the Word our final authority in life.

When we hear God's Word, we receive His faith. When we hear Satan's words, we receive his fear. It is all about whom we are listening to! If we are going to live by faith, we must listen to God more than we do the enemy. This is what it means to live a life of faith.

In today's turbulent, fear-filled world, we must hold on to the only thing that can deliver us from fear—the Word of God. It is our protection, deliverance, and security. Psalm 91 is my daily meditation where these issues are concerned. I confess it, knowing I have unseen assistants—angels—enforcing the salvation that is available to me through Jesus Christ. I live a life full of faith by trusting, believing, and acting on the Word. What about you? Have you allowed the cares of this world to cloud your vision of God's unchanging Word? Have words of doubt, fear, and unbelief crept into your heart? Take inventory. Recognize that fear tolerated is faith contaminated. God has already destroyed the power of death and the bondage that comes through fear. Dare to take your place in God's kingdom as a fearless believer.

SECTION FOUR

WINNING OVER ADDICTIVE BEHAVIORS

DECLARING WAR ON LUST

By understanding what lust is, its purpose, and how to defeat it from a spiritual and practical standpoint, we are assured victory.

It is the unquenchable desire that is never satisfied, the strong appetite for something outside the boundaries of God's Word. It is the driving impulse behind addictive behaviors. It is *lust*, and it destroys lives. So many people deal with lust but have no idea how to overcome it. They try to break habits through willpower, only to fall prey to the same temptations over and over again. Patterns of addiction are hard to break without God's power operating in our lives. Obtaining freedom from lust is probably one of the most challenging tasks a person will face, but it can be done. By understanding what lust is, its purpose, and how to defeat it from a spiritual *and* practical standpoint, we are assured victory.

Lust is one of those topics that is not often taught on or discussed in Christian circles, even though so many believers are struggling with it in their lives. Marriages and friendships have been destroyed because of it. And the morals and values of society have been compromised by it. I am determined to address the critical issues in which people need help, and this is definitely one of them.

Satan is never obvious with the tactics he uses to entice us into harmful behavior; he is the master of subtlety. He will try to get us in position to receive seeds of lust without us even realizing it.

Many times, it is not until we are in the grip of an addiction that we realize something is desperately wrong. So how do we break free from lust forever? By recognizing how it gets in us, and knowing how to get it out.

The entertainment industry is one very effective tool the enemy constantly uses to influence the general public. Fear, sexual lust, and a host of other negative emotions are easily deposited in the subconscious mind through movies, television programs, and music. In addition, friends and associates also influence our mind-sets, habits, and behavior. It does not matter how old you are; *anyone* can fall prey to lust if certain words and images are allowed into the heart.

DESIGNED TO DESTROY

Lust has one purpose, and one purpose only—to move us out of the will of God for our lives. The enemy does not want the power of God to work for us, in us, or through us; and he knows lust will absolutely short-circuit that power. So he works overtime to get us to receive lustful thoughts and act on them. His whole objective is to steal, kill, and destroy.

What is lust? It is any desire that is outside the will of God and outside the boundaries of the Word of God. It is an intense appetite or longing for something. Don't get me wrong, desire in and of itself is not bad. In fact, God gave us natural, healthy desires. Some examples are the desire for food and water, and the desire to be unconditionally loved and accepted. Sex is a desire as well, but when the desire for sex outside the context of marriage begins dominating a person's thinking, that desire has turned into lust.

Lust is not limited to only sex. It can affect virtually *any* desire we have. This is all too common in the area of eating. God put a natural desire for food in all of us, not only for our physiological needs but also for our pleasure and enjoyment! However, when the desire for food becomes all-consuming and drives us to crave it above and beyond what our body needs for optimum health, it becomes gluttony. This includes eating when we are not hungry, overeating, and feeding the cravings and tastes we've created for food that is bad for us. Eating habits that are driven by lust, just like lustful sexual desires, can destroy our health and send us to an early grave. The same is true about the desire for money, power, and even relationships. Any desire taken out of its proper context is lustful and destructive.

How does lust become sin? James 1:15 says, "Then when lust hath conceived, it bringeth forth sin: and sin, when it is finished, bringeth forth death." The progression here is very clear. First, lust is conceived or planted in the heart. After it is conceived and nourished, it inevitably produces sin in our lives. And sin, when it has run its course, ultimately leads to spiritual death. Lust is designed to kill us, plain and simple.

The progression of lust is evident all around us. Our world is full of it. The Bible sums up this present world's condition in three ways: the lust of the eyes, the lust of the flesh, and the pride of life (see 1 John 2:16). The norms and values of society today actually support and encourage ungodly appetites and desires. It is everywhere you turn—from reality television shows to popular music.

I think we all know someone who is or was ruled by lustful desires. Some of us may even have family members and close friends who have died because they could never conquer the cravings that controlled their lives. Just as a fire needs wood in order to keep burning, the same is true with lust. It will not stop until its victim is completely consumed.

HOW LUST IS CONCEIVED

I believe if we can locate how lust gets into our hearts, we can take action against it from the start. James 1:14 says something very interesting: "But every man is tempted, when he is drawn away of his own lust, and enticed." This Scripture is key because it dispels the myth that the devil *makes* us engage in lustful behavior. While there is no denying the fact that ungodly influences are all around us, the Scripture makes it plain that once lust is allowed into a person's heart, as an act of his or her will, *it becomes his or her own*. It is like a baby who is nurtured and fed until he grows up to be big and strong.

Once lust is in a person's heart, the enemy will entice him or her to feed and nurture that seed by presenting people, ideas, images, and situations that appeal to the lust that is already present. These things act as a type of bait designed to tempt the person to act on his or her desires. Once the desire is acted upon, the cycle of sin is activated. The temporary pleasure attached to the sin blinds the person to the truth that he or she is on a collision course with death. This is how Satan destroys people's lives. He will never stop making presentations, so it now becomes *our* responsibility to resist his suggestions so lust never gets the opportunity to get inside of us.

I often say that what you give attention to is what you will desire. And what you look at, listen to, and meditate on—when acted upon—will overwhelm and overtake your life. Lust gets into our lives through the three gates to our hearts—the eyes, the ears, and the mouth. If you spend all your time listening to music that talks about sex, or looking at graphic images, eventually you will begin to desire them. You cannot afford to flirt with things like pornography and sexually explicit materials. If you have never looked at these things, don't start now! Doing so will only create a battle with your spirit and soul that you do not want to have to deal with (1 Peter 2:11).

Proverbs 4:23 states, "Keep thy heart with all diligence; for out of it are the issues of life." The issues of life are the things that have the potential to overpower us. These forces can either be good or bad. The "heart" refers to the spirit of a man—that part of us that is re-created when we accept Jesus Christ as our Lord and Savior. The heart is the unseen core of every person, and it is responsible for growing the seeds we plant there.

For example, if we constantly read, meditate on, and speak the Word of God, it will begin to take root deep within us, and it will produce a harvest of peace, joy, faith, and prosperity. We will begin acting in ways that reflect God and His way of doing things. We will begin to receive the mind of Christ. So likewise, when we allow seeds of lust to enter our hearts through our eyes, ears, and mouth (the words we speak), the same thing will happen in the negative. We will receive the mind of Satan and begin acting in a way that pleases him, not God.

As we look at the life of David, we find an example of how lust, when conceived in a man's heart, leads to disastrous consequences. Second Samuel 11:1–4 gives the account of David and Bathsheba:

And it came to pass, after the year was expired, at the time when kings go forth to battle, that David sent Joab, and his servants with him, and all Israel; and they destroyed the children of Ammon, and besieged Rabbah. But David tarried still at Jerusalem. And it came to pass in an eveningtide, that David arose from off his bed, and walked upon the roof of the king's house: and from the roof he saw a woman washing herself; and the woman was very beautiful to look upon. And David sent and enquired after the woman. And one said, Is not this Bathsheba, the daughter of Eliam, the wife of Uriah the Hittite? And David sent messengers, and took her; and she came in unto him, and he lay with her.

In this story, we see the king allowing his eyes to linger a little too long on someone he had no business giving attention to. Bathsheba was a married woman. We do not know what was going on in David and Bathsheba's lives at the time of the affair, but we do know the Word says David saw this naked woman and noticed her beauty. He was driven by lust to the point where he overrode every godly impulse in his heart and sent for her.

The events that followed are classic examples of how one seed of lust that is conceived and acted upon can result in a chain of events that spiral out of control. Bathsheba ended up getting pregnant. To keep her husband from finding out about it, David had him killed on the battlefield (2 Samuel 11:15). The Word says what he did displeased God (verse 27). Even though David repented, there were far-reaching consequences for his actions.

Another example of lust's destructive influences is found in the life of Amnon, David's son, and his lust for his sister, Tamar. "And it came to pass after this, that Absalom the son of David had a fair sister, whose name was Tamar; and Amnon the son of David loved her. And Amnon was so vexed, that he fell sick for his sister Tamar; for she was a virgin; and Amnon thought it hard for him to do any thing to her" (2 Samuel 13:1–2).

Amnon had allowed lust to creep into his heart to such a point that it actually drove him to rape her (2 Samuel 13:14). Amnon ended up paying for his actions with his life. He was killed by his brother Absalom out of vengeance for what he'd done.

The lust for power ended up costing Absalom his life. In an attempt to usurp his father's power to become king over the people, he led a revolt against King David. In the end, however, Absalom was killed (2 Samuel 18:14–15).

David lost two of his sons because of actions driven by lust. And I believe the seed of generational lust was planted when David gave in to his own ungodly desires with Bathsheba. Lust always has a price tag attached to it.

I remember being exposed to lustful ways of thinking when I was younger. My family members had no qualms about schooling me on women, sex, and how to handle myself in these relationships. As a result, I grew up with a lot of wrong ideas about these things. I came from a family where, for as long as I can remember, all of the men had extramarital affairs. From uncles to cousins, if they were not actually involved in some type of sexual affair, they were talking about what they were *going* to do. And the young men in my family were encouraged, from an early age, to "get some" (have sex). In fact, I had relatives tell me, "Boy, if you don't have sex by the time you're fifteen, we're gonna buy you some."

Well, I got to a certain point in my life where I made the decision to stop this generational curse of lust. I said to myself, *The woman I marry is the woman I will love and cherish, and I will not invite another person to partake of that relationship.* I had seen the damaging effects of extramarital affairs—the hurt, pain, and broken family relationships. I did not want any of that invading my household or affecting my children.

I can recall going to a Bible study while I was in college and hearing the speaker talk about fornication. To be honest, I had never even heard of the word! I had no idea up to that point that having sex outside of marriage was wrong. Once I learned the truth about it, I began to renew my mind in this area. I discovered that lust is at the root of fornication, and it is not the will of God to get involved in premarital or extramarital sex. Gaining understanding about this issue allowed me to receive revelation concerning lust and obtain victory over it.

CONSEQUENCES OF AN UNRESTRAINED LIFE

The sin you fail to deal with will eventually end up dealing with you. What seems like a harmlessly pleasurable act at first can quickly spin out of control. When lustful desires are continually acted upon, with no repentance or attempt to curb the behavior, a person can easily get into what is called *lasciviousness*, which involves having no self-control.

Lasciviousness is a work of the flesh, and it is the result of allowing the wrong things into our hearts. It can be defined as *wantonness or negligence of restraint; an unrestrained life, immorality.* It occurs when pressure is applied to your flesh, causing that ungodly mind-set to grow and dominate your spirit. Another characteristic of lasciviousness is the inability to find the brakes to stop engaging in certain behavior. It is a cycle that starts in our lives as a result of neglecting the fundamental truths of God's Word and allowing lust to rule our lives.

Remember, the flesh is a mind-set that opposes the Word. Our bodies do only what we tell them to do. When the flesh is dominating a person's soul (mind, will, and emotions), his or her spirit is at its weakest point. And it won't be long before he or she yields to the impulses and desires that have been consistently nourished. On the other hand, when we starve the flesh—meaning we do not feed our carnal nature with images, words, and conversations that create lustful desires—but instead feed our spirits the Word of God, our actions will be dictated by a godly mind-set.

God never intended for the carnal nature to direct our lives. Galatians 6:8 says when we sow to the flesh, we will reap corruption; but when we sow to the Spirit, we will reap a harvest of everlasting life. There is no way around the truth that living a lust-ruled life will result in destruction. But how do we become free of it once certain desires have been turned on?

First, I believe it takes being really honest with ourselves. We must first identify those areas where our flesh is weak. When we are born again, our spirits are re-created, but our souls are not. Our minds must be renewed on a daily basis to embrace God's way of doing things.

All people have certain areas in which they may have a tendency to fall into sin, and it is in these areas the enemy will always try to tempt us. He has what I call a "file" that contains every area where he used to have control. Locating and being honest about our strengths and weaknesses is the first step toward developing an action plan to eradicate lust and lasciviousness.

For example, if food is your weakness, then it will be the very thing the enemy will use to weaken your resolve and dominate your flesh. The same is true for sex, drugs, uncontrolled spending, and any other addictive behavior. So now you must ask yourself, *Where is my weak area?* Your answer will let you know where you have to do the most work and where you must initiate the most safeguards.

Once we identify where lust and lasciviousness have taken over, we must take swift, decisive action and starve the desire, while simultaneously forcing our minds to come under subjection to the Word of God. Keep in mind, lasciviousness never just shows up out of nowhere. It begins with a thought or suggestion from the enemy that we fail to cast out of our minds. And if we fail to exercise restraint where our thoughts are concerned, we open ourselves up to lust.

Consequently, we must become vigilant custodians over our thought lives if we are to ever see victory in these areas. We cannot just sit idly by while the devil bombards us with lustful thoughts and images. We have to fight back!

Second Corinthians 10:4–5 says, "(For the weapons of our warfare are not carnal, but mighty through God to the pulling down of strong holds;) Casting down imaginations, and every high thing that exalteth itself against the knowledge of God, and bringing into captivity every thought to the obedience of Christ."

I can already hear someone saying, "It is impossible to control your thoughts." This is simply not true. Brother Kenneth Hagin, a great man of God, once said, "You can't stop the birds from flying over your head, but you can keep them from building a nest in your hair." In other words, though the thoughts will come, we do not have to accept them. We can cast thoughts down and destroy mental strongholds by speaking the Word of God *every* time a thought comes to our minds.

This is particularly important when trying to break free from addiction. We know the contradictory thoughts are going to come quickly and consistently. This simply means we must be that much more aggressive with our confessions. I don't care if you have to cast down thoughts five hundred times a day—do what you have to do! Open your mouth and cancel lustful thinking by declaring what God has said. His Word is powerful, and it never fails.

As you continue to practice casting down thoughts, something powerful will begin to happen. Not only will it become easier to get rid of the mind-sets that have been defeating you, but you will discover your mind beginning to align with the principles of the Word of God. The more you confess the Word, the more you hear it, which then causes it to become planted in your heart and produce faith. As that Word becomes a part of your spirit and soul, your desires will begin to change.

Romans 12:1–2 advises us to not be conformed to the world's way of thinking, but to renew our minds so we can prove the acceptable will of God. We know that lust is not of God. In order for us to demonstrate what the perfect will of God is, our thinking must be transformed to agree with Him. Renewing our minds is a daily process that takes place as we continually meditate on the Word and act on it. Every time we obey what God says rather than what our flesh says, we renew our minds. Every temptation you say no to, in favor of what pleases God, puts you that much farther ahead. As you act on the Word and saturate your mind with it, you will begin living a life that is pleasing to Him.

As I mentioned earlier, it is critical to literally cut off the source of your addiction. This is the practical aspect of deliverance many people fail to do, and then they wonder why they are entangled again in their old behavior. I cannot stress how important it is to starve the lust in your life. If it is a certain type of food you crave, get rid of anything in your house that caters to that desire and stay away from it at all costs! If sex is your issue, cut off contact with your sex partners; change your phone number if you have to. Separate yourself from anyone and anything that helps support your addiction. Without taking essential, practical steps, all your spiritual efforts are in vain.

DEVELOPING TEMPERANCE AS A WAY OF LIFE

As we now know, lasciviousness is the result of lust and is a work of the flesh. Temperance is just the opposite. It is a fruit of the Spirit and an antidote for a life of no restraint (Galatians 5:22–23). Neglecting to cultivate temperance in our lives opens the door to lasciviousness.

When we talk about adding restraints to our lives, the truth is, no one really wants to do it. However, it is necessary because where there is a lack of restraint, lasciviousness is formed. We must work daily to do the things necessary to curb the desires we know are not good for us.

In my own life I have really had to apply temperance where my eating is concerned. There was a time when I had absolutely no self-control when it came to eating sweets, specifically apple pie. I used to eat a whole pie in one sitting. It eventually got to the point where I was hiding snack pies all over the house to eat at my leisure! Then, after eating a pie one day, my entire leg began to throb with pain. The large amount of sugar I was consuming was starting to take a toll on my body. I knew if I did not get control over my lust for apple pie, my health would be threatened. I had to put some restraints in place quickly!

Eating healthy and changing my taste for certain foods was not easy, but I had to look at the bigger picture. God needs me to be alive so I can complete His will for my life in excellence. Eating large quantities of sweets and other unhealthy food was doing nothing to prolong my life and protect my body from disease. So many people die prematurely because they fail to develop temperance in some area of their lives, and it destroys them. I did not want to be counted in that number. For this reason, I made the necessary adjustments in this area of weakness in my life.

I have discovered you have to *want* to be free in order to obtain freedom. Everyone is simply not willing to pay the price. Breaking addictions that are born out of lust is not easy. You must be strong and committed to eradicating these behaviors, no matter what it takes. So: How badly do you want change? What area of your life is causing you to slip, time and time again? Where has lust infiltrated your heart and polluted your thinking? Locate yourself and be honest. Ask God to assist you in your process of deliverance, and He will.

I want to encourage you to refuse to allow your life to be ruled by lust. God has created you for a great purpose—a purpose that transcends any type of lustful fantasy or behavior. His plan is for you to prosper and experience success *His* way. Winning the battle over lust takes determination, but the rewards are well worth it.

OVERCOMING 20 SELFISHNESS

Selfishness hinders the power of God from operating in our lives to its fullest capacity.

⟨⟩⟨⟩ There is a key to winning in troubled times that most people do not consider, but it is the most vital component of victory. It is one of the most powerful forces on the planet and is *guaranteed* to put us in a winning position. It is love. If we can get our love walk in line, we can achieve unprecedented results in our relationships, finances, family, and personal lives. However, in order for love to have free reign, we must deal with selfishness, which hinders the power of God from operating in our lives to its fullest capacity.

Love and selfishness are the two most powerful forces on earth. And everything we do is fueled by one of the two. Sin is based on selfishness, while all the principles and benefits of the Word of God are based on love. Without love in operation, God cannot accomplish His plans; and without selfishness, the devil cannot fulfill his.

First Corinthians 13 is the Bible's love chapter because it describes all the characteristics of love, giving a clear outline of what demonstrates the love of God and what doesn't. Verses 4–8 say: "Love is patient, love is kind. It does not envy, it does not boast, it is not proud. It is not rude, it is not self-seeking, it is not easily angered, it keeps no record of wrongs. Love does not delight in evil but rejoices with the truth. It always protects, always trusts, always hopes, always perseveres. Love never fails" (NIV).

I like to refer back to this passage frequently because it reminds me of how my love walk should be. Whenever I find myself slipping into a bad attitude or negative emotions toward situations and people, I remind myself of 1 Corinthians 13. It is the bedrock for the Christian life.

What is true, Bible-based love that reflects God's character? It is essentially giving of yourself unconditionally. It is extending forgiveness with no strings attached, despite how badly you've been hurt. It is loving those who have wronged you, hurt you, and made you angry. It is loving without reservations, not because you feel like it, but because God commanded you to.

Genuine love is focused on meeting the needs of others before our own and is more concerned with giving someone else the advantage rather than taking advantage. It is one of those subjects a lot of people do not really want to hear about because it challenges them to look at their lives and examine their own motives and actions.

First Corinthians 13:8 says, "Love never fails" (NIV). Love never fails because God *is* love (see 1 John 4:16), and *God* never fails. Everything from speaking in tongues to prophecy will eventually pass away. But not love; it is the preeminent force.

In Matthew 22:35–40, Jesus speaks about how love drives everything in the kingdom of God:

> Then one of them, which was a lawyer, asked him a question, tempting him, and saying, Master, which is the great commandment in the law? Jesus said unto him, Thou shalt love the Lord thy God with all thy heart, and with all thy soul, and with all thy mind. This is the first and great commandment. And the second is like unto it, Thou shalt love thy neighbour as thyself. On these two commandments hang all the law and the prophets.

We are first to love God with everything we have, and everything within us, and then we are to love our neighbor as ourselves.

These two commandments cover every law and principle found in the Word.

Galatians 5:22–23 reveals the components of the love walk. "But the fruit of the Spirit is love, joy, peace, longsuffering, gentleness, goodness, faith, meekness, temperance: against such there is no law." These characteristics describe what it means to walk in love. So if we want to measure the development of love in our lives, it can be determined by the extent to which these qualities are evident.

Ask yourself: *Do I have self-control? Am I patient and kind? Do I operate in faith?* If any of the love "segments" are not present in your life, your love walk is out of balance and there is some form of selfishness taking place.

THE ORIGIN OF SELFISHNESS

Selfishness originated with Satan, formerly known as Lucifer. Before he was cast out of heaven, Lucifer was the most beautiful angel God created. He was an *archangel* who was charged with overseeing praise, worship, and everything pertaining to music in heaven. But Lucifer took things too far; he began to have a higher estimation of himself than he should have. He started to exalt himself, his plans, his desires, and his pursuits above the will of God.

Ezekiel 28:14–17 paints the picture of the position Lucifer held until he allowed selfishness to corrupt him. God describes him as the "anointed cherub that covers." But the moment corruption was found in him, he was cast out of heaven. This is because love and selfishness cannot coexist. God would not allow Lucifer's selfish motives to pollute the atmosphere of love.

Lucifer was so perfect, beautiful, and flawless that pride and vanity crept into him. Once that happened, he took his focus off of God and put it on himself. His conceit was so intense that in

Isaiah 14:13–14 he declared, "I will exalt my throne above the stars of God…I will be like the most High." He became completely consumed with himself and even deceived a third of the angels in heaven by getting them to focus on themselves, too. But in the end, selfishness cost him everything. He was ultimately separated from God. Likewise, when you become the focus of everything, you create a platform for sin in your life. Being selfish demonstrates the character of Satan, not God, and only love can extinguish selfish emotions.

LOVE VERSUS SELFISHNESS

I think it is important to distinguish the difference between the love that reflects the character of God and carnal, emotional love. The world's idea of love is actually based on selfishness. It is the love we see on television shows and movies. This type of love is born out of emotions and is always looking for a reward, payback, or recognition. It says, "I'll love you as long as you do this for me. As long as things feel good, I will love you." It has strings attached. Unfortunately, because it is selfish and carnal, it quickly fades when it doesn't get its way.

One of the most familiar scenarios where emotional, selfish love is demonstrated is in marriage relationships. I believe one of the reasons the divorce rate is so high today is because people are getting married without a true understanding of what love really is. Instead, they are coming into the relationship with fantasies, false expectations, and most of all—selfishness. They do not realize love is not a feeling; it is a decision. And the decision to love according to God's example gives us the ability to remain committed to our marriages, regardless of how we feel.

Selfishness can be defined as being "concerned excessively… with oneself…without regard for others," self-centered; self-seeking.[1]

The selfish person is the one who is living for himself and fulfilling his own interests, whether or not those interests coincide with God's will or not. He is more concerned with obtaining what he wants and desires. The selfish person is completely focused on pleasing himself at any cost.

Selfishness is rooted in fear. Therefore, selfish individuals are fearful people. Selfishness is a result of the deeply rooted fear they have of coming up short in some area. They become easy prey for the enemy as they get into what I call "self-preservation." Instead of trusting God to provide for their needs in a particular area, they trust in their own abilities. They think they know a better way—their own way. Selfish people fear they may somehow be taken advantage of or end up on the losing end of the deal. Consequently, they become protective of the little they do have and try to hold on to it for dear life.

Selfishness is not limited to only the material realm. Usually, when we think of a selfish person, we get the picture of someone who is stingy with his or her personal belongings. While this is a common area of selfishness, a person can be selfish emotionally as well. Not wanting to give of your time or not wanting to help someone in need is just as reflective of selfishness as not sharing your material resources. Any time you are solely focused on yourself in *any* area, selfishness is involved.

Galatians 5:19–21 describes the works of the flesh, which are the results of selfishness. Sexual sin, idolatry, witchcraft, hatred, strife, and a host of other behaviors are all built on a platform of selfishness, which is why these things are often so difficult to give up. Wherever you find selfishness, you will find protectiveness over those areas that are pleasurable. When we are selfish, we want to preserve what makes us feel good, even though our habits and actions may be hurting us and other people. Selfish people cannot see past the present moment or the big picture.

As I stated before, I used to have a serious issue where my temper was concerned. I would fly off the handle in a heartbeat and say things that were very hurtful. Angry outbursts were the normal way I responded to situations and people who ticked me off. When I really began to look at my behavior, I realized I was walking in selfishness. Yes, it felt good to my flesh to cuss someone out and let them have it. But it was hurting those I cared about. I didn't realize at the time that my anger was actually based in fear of not being in control. My angry outbursts were an expression of self-preservation. I was threatened by any circumstance that would make me look like I did not have a handle on everything.

I began to implement some guidelines where my mouth was concerned to help me stay on target with my goal to develop self-control. I told God I would put a "bit" in my mouth to keep me from saying things out of anger that would hurt others. I was committed to defeating this area of selfishness in my life.

Can you locate selfishness in the way you think, speak, and act toward others? Are your fleshly desires hindering your spiritual growth? Everyone has room to improve. Through my study of God's love, I began to see how the selfish acts described in Galatians 5:19–21 can actually be counteracted with the fruit of the Spirit—love. It takes a conscious decision. Every sin and work of the flesh can be linked back to selfishness, which can be cancelled by releasing the love of God. There is no selfishness in love.

NOTHING JUST HAPPENS

Many of the negative things that take place in our lives happen because we turn on certain laws through our choices. And those choices end up taking us in the wrong direction. I know this is not easy to hear, but it is the truth. The devil can only do so much; he has only as much access as we give him in our lives. Nothing just happens.

That being said, every Christian needs to be aware of the two laws mentioned in chapter 14 that are operating in the earth at all times—the law of the Spirit of life in Christ Jesus and the law of sin and death. When either of these two laws is activated, certain things take place. If we are operating in the law of life in Christ Jesus, the fruit of activating that law is love. But if we are operating in the law of sin and death, selfishness is the outcome.

The significance of these two laws is that the love and selfishness produced by each one give birth to faith and fear respectively. So if you want to know if selfishness is alive in your life, simply identify any fear you may have. Similarly, faith operating in your heart is evidence that the love of God is present.

The law of the Spirit of life in Christ Jesus has already made us free from the law of sin and death (Romans 8:2)! This simply means we do not have to be in bondage to selfishness and fear because of the preeminent power of Christ's law. All we have to do is turn it on by walking in the love of God and abandoning the desires of the flesh. The law of the Spirit of life in Christ Jesus will set you free from selfishness forever.

Now, there are two specific things we must do to defeat selfishness in our lives. The first is to develop a God-consciousness and the second is to allow perfected love to flush fear out of our hearts. When these two components are working, selfishness doesn't stand a chance.

Developing a God-consciousness is a major key because it is what gets us out of self-preservation mode. In the beginning, when God created mankind, He imparted His life into them. They came out of God and were connected to Him. Adam and Eve were aware of God at all times and enjoyed the benefits of uninterrupted fellowship with Him.

Unfortunately, Satan wanted to dismantle the relationship between God and His family, so he tried to get them to take their focus off God and put it on themselves. Sadly, his plan worked. By yielding to the enemy's suggestions and temptations, Adam and Eve lost focus of what was important—what God had said to them. Once their attention was diverted, they were no longer

God-conscious, but self-conscious. As a result, they hid from the
only Father they knew up to that point.

Adam and Eve's self-consciousness threw them into an existence of self-preservation. Before, they had no idea their bodies
were not clothed, but as soon as they became self-conscious, they
tried to cover themselves with fig leaves (Genesis 3:7). Before,
they had no thoughts of having to work for what they needed.
They depended solely on God and received everything they
needed from Him, without thought or care. But becoming aware
of self placed them in a different position. They lost their connection with the Father, and selfishness emerged.

As we look at what happened to Adam and Eve, it becomes clear
why it is so vital that we maintain our connection with God at all
times. Spending time in God's Word gives us power to shut out
the whispers of Satan. Our hope comes from the Word, and if we
neglect meditating on it and speaking it, we run the risk of slipping into selfishness. God wants us to get our focus off ourselves
and put it on Him.

Matthew 6:31–32 gives a great example of how we should look
at life: "Therefore take no thought, saying, What shall we eat? or,
What shall we drink? or, Wherewithal shall we be clothed? (For
after all these things do the Gentiles seek:) For your heavenly
Father knoweth that ye have need of all these things."

Self-preservation becomes particularly evident when it comes
to getting our needs met. In today's world, fear is at an all-time
high where finances and provision are concerned. If we are not
careful, we will begin to look at the things going on around us
and take our focus off God, who is the Source of all our supply. A
fear of lack automatically produces selfishness, which may manifest itself as hoarding and stinginess.

But when we give more attention to what God says here in this
passage—that He knows we have need of food, clothing, and
provisions, and we should not even accept one thought saying
otherwise—we are free to give our resources, knowing our giving

positions us to receive what we need. This is just one example of what it means to be God-conscious rather than self-conscious. Anytime you find yourself getting into selfishness, it is time to shift your focus back to God and start practicing His presence.

The second way to overcome selfishness is to allow perfected love to operate in your life. We've looked at this before, but let's look again: "There is no fear in love; but perfect love casteth out fear: because fear hath torment. He that feareth is not made perfect in love" (1 John 4:18). Fear and selfishness go hand in hand. Since perfected love casts out fear, selfishness also has to go.

When the Word talks about *perfected* love it means *developed* or mature love. How do we perfect love? By cultivating the fruit of the Spirit—joy, peace, long-suffering, gentleness, goodness, faith, meekness, and temperance. I'm sure you've heard the saying, "Practice makes perfect." Well, when you practice loving others, having self-control, being patient, kind, and gentle, you become more developed in the love of God. Consequently, you begin to mature in it, and it is perfected in your life. The more this godly love begins to grow on the inside of you, the more God-conscious and selfless you will become. You will start looking for ways to bless others.

We will have plenty of opportunities to perfect the love of God. I believe He wants us to be in relationships with people for this very reason. It is during the challenging times in these relationships that we grow in the love of God. Instead of running from the challenge, embrace it, by allowing your "love muscle" to be developed!

This principle of allowing the love of God to be perfected in us is not limited to only intimate relationships. It applies to relationships with our children, coworkers, and friends as well. There are always opportunities to be more loving. Remember, love *never* fails.

The *agape* love of God is so powerful because nothing the enemy brings to us can stand against it. If anger, irritation, and frustration are affecting your mind, the answer is to love *more* aggressively. If we start living this way, we can destroy Satan's schemes. He will not be able to keep you broke, sick, and burdened down with strife, bitterness, and unforgiveness. Stress won't even be able to get a foothold in your life because you will realize it's not all about you anyway! When you are love-conscious, you will say, "Lord, I cast my cares on You because you care for me."

I have been on this love journey for years, and I cannot tell you the impact the love of God has made in my life. My relationships and responsibilities have been simplified just by getting rid of selfishness and making love a priority. As Christians, we have the love of God operating on the inside of us—the same love God has toward Jesus and the same ability to love that Jesus has. If you are struggling in your relationships, finances, or even on your job, make a commitment to change your perspective. Allow the *agape* love of God to escort you away *from yourself*, so you can conquer the spirit of selfishness. Your life will never be the same!

CONCLUSION

IT'S TIME TO MAKE A WINNING CHANGE

We must manage our lives from a spiritual perspective. When we can master our spirit, our soul and body will follow.

ﾟﾟﾟ Change is not easy. I know because I have had to make a lot of adjustments in my life over the years in areas that were extremely difficult. From eating habits to anger, I know what it means to dig in and transform what has become a comfortable norm. However, change is essential as we reach for God's best in our lives. It is the evidence that we are growing and developing as individuals. And true and lasting change occurs only when we are committed to renewing our minds.

If you are growing, you should be changing. Where there is no change, growth is at a standstill. When I talk about changing things about ourselves that stifle our growth and progress, it makes people uncomfortable, especially when we are so accustomed to our set behavior patterns. It becomes a real task to break the mold and go against what has become normal for us. Nevertheless, change is as inevitable as the changing of leaves with each new season. Whether you choose to accept it or not, it is happening all the time.

Here I will share the five Rs that will cause change. These steps will work in your marriage, finances, physical health, and in raising your children. If you make it a point to act on them, they can bring lasting change.

When we talk about change, the first place to start is in the Word of God, which is the only reliable reference on how to transform our thinking and keep it on the right track. Romans 12:1–2 gives the formula for how to initiate the process of change and keep it going. In the Amplified Bible it reads:

> I appeal to you therefore, brethren, and beg of you in view of [all] the mercies of God, to make a decisive dedication of your bodies [presenting all your members and faculties] as a living sacrifice, holy (devoted, consecrated) and well pleasing to God, which is your reasonable (rational, intelligent) service and spiritual worship. Do not be conformed to this world (this age), [fashioned after and adapted to its external, superficial customs], but be transformed (changed) by the [entire] renewal of your mind [by its new ideals and its new attitude], so that you may prove [for yourselves] what is the good and acceptable and perfect will of God, even the thing which is good and acceptable and perfect [in His sight for you].

Interestingly, Paul starts this passage off urging believers to dedicate their physical bodies to God. So clearly, what we do with our bodies is important to the Lord. When you present your body as a living sacrifice, you are saying, *I am not going to allow my body to be used for things that go against the Word of God.*

This part of the Scripture speaks directly to the addictions that have to do with sins of the body, such as fornication and adultery. When we engage in illicit sex, we are essentially violating God's dwelling place. He lives in us, and our bodies belong not to us but to Him. When we commit sexual sins, we sin against our own bodies (1 Corinthians 6:13, 18).

Paul is emphasizing the connection between renewing the

mind and what we do with our bodies. You see, the body does only what the mind tells it to do; it does not act independently. So, whatever is governing the way we think is going to eventually govern what we do with our bodies. The apostle Paul was speaking to Christians, so clearly he was dealing with church folks who had challenges controlling their physical urges. Has anything changed today? People, Christians included, are still using their bodies to worship their addictions and ungodly behaviors rather than to worship God, which is why a change of mind-set is so vital.

So he goes on to say we should not be conformed to the world's way of doing things. This is really the core issue when it comes to changing. The fact is, we live in a world that clings to beliefs that contradict the Word of God. Many norms and values in our society are in direct opposition to God's will. And most of us grew up learning these mind-sets from an early age. Parents, friends, and associates helped shape the way we think and believe. Still others of us have been reared in "religious" households, where we went to church but had no revelation of how to execute the principles of the Word in our daily lives.

Because we are surrounded by and indoctrinated with worldly beliefs about the issues of life, it becomes critical that we constantly receive new insight from the Word to reset our thinking. Instead of being conformed to the world, we are to focus on being transformed by renewing our minds. When something is *renewed*, it is restored or made new again. Before Adam and Eve sinned in the Garden of Eden, their minds were infused with the life of God. They were able to connect with Him—spirit, soul, and body. But when they disobeyed Him, by eating the fruit of the forbidden tree, they connected with the curse. They became emotionally ruled as their minds were darkened by the law of sin and death, which began to dominate their thinking.

However, through Jesus Christ, we are no longer subject to cursed thinking. We are now able to reconnect with the power that has the ability to restore our minds to their original state of peace, wholeness, and agreement with God. The Word is the bridge that makes this renewal possible.

Only by changing our thinking to align with God's Word can we even begin to see, comprehend, and apply the Word to our lives. This is what it means to prove *for ourselves* what the perfect will of God is. As we renew our minds, we become convinced and secure that God's Word is truth, and it is the final authority in our lives.

Renewing the mind is not a onetime event; it is a lifetime process. Neither is it simply introducing new knowledge to our minds. A renewed mind is evidenced in a man or a woman's life when old temptations are ineffective. Because they have a new way of thinking, new ideas, and a new attitude about that particular area, the old temptation cannot match up to their new mindset. But if we maintain our same old thought patterns, even if we receive a lot of new information, real change will not take place. Learning, by itself, will not cause the change; applying and acting on what we learn will.

Many times people fail to realize that when it comes to overcoming addictions, they must make a commitment to *continually* feed their minds the Word of God. The biggest deception is believing that once we see some results or change, we can scale back on the time we spend in the Word. On the contrary, we have to decide that we will continue to renew our minds for the rest of our lives and do just that.

THE FIVE Rs OF CHANGE

Michael Jackson sang a song titled "Man in the Mirror," which talks about looking in the mirror and, starting with ourselves, really making change take place in our lives and in the world around us. Looking at your reflection gives you the clearest picture of what you really look like. But if you could not see how you looked, you would have no clue as to whether you needed to comb your hair or put on makeup. Just as we look in the mirror to adjust our appearance, we must look at ourselves through the mirror of the Word, take full responsibility for where we are, and make the necessary adjustments.

The First R: Responsibility

The first R of change is probably one of the most difficult, simply because it pulls the rug out from under any and all excuses. It is *responsibility.* Now, I cannot tell you how important this is where change is concerned. Our current situation in life is the result of decisions we have made. We cannot blame God, our spouses, our neighbors, our employers, or anyone else. Until we take full responsibility, we will remain out of control and incapable of changing.

What happens when a person says, "I accept full responsibility for myself and for my life"? What he is saying, in essence, is: "I accept full responsibility to change." But when he continues to play the blame game, he demonstrates he is unwilling to make the necessary adjustments to see results in his life. It is so much easier to blame an outside source rather than take responsibility for the role we have played in our own personal dramas in life.

A few years back, I mentored a young man who had issues with drug addiction. After some time, he had gotten clean and was doing well. All of a sudden, he disappeared for a while, and during that time he ended up relapsing. When he came back to church, he told me he was actually mad at me, and that it was *my* fault that he started doing drugs again. I was shocked! What he was clearly saying was, *I'm blaming you because of my refusal to change myself.* The truth is, he was solely responsible for his addiction, and no one else.

Another person we tend to blame when things go wrong is the

devil. Now, we know the devil is real, and that he is constantly working to wreak havoc in our lives. His goal is to steal, kill, and destroy, but he cannot do anything unless we take his bait. Yet I see so many Christians blaming Satan for situations and circumstances *they* created. The enemy cannot invade our lives without our permission on some level. And even when he does try to come against us, we can use the authority of God's Word to put him on the run.

The area of finances is one area where people really put more blame on the enemy than he deserves. The truth of the matter is, most people are in financial dilemmas because of their own bad habits. If we really begin to examine our bank accounts, we can usually trace the problem back to spending addictions and living beyond our means. When our expenses exceed our income, we set ourselves up for financial challenges. The devil cannot be blamed for our faulty decisions.

The same is true in marriage and family matters. Something powerful happens when you say, "I'm responsible for where this marriage is. I'm responsible for why my kids are acting this way. My selfishness has brought me to this point." No one else can be blamed for where we are.

Responsibility is *management*. We must manage our lives from a spiritual perspective. When we can master our spirit, our soul and body will follow.

Hebrews 4:12 talks about how the Word of God is sharper than a two-edged sword, and it divides the line between the spirit and the soul. From this Scripture, we can conclude that only God's Word can penetrate deep into a man's innermost being. It is the only thing that can cause real change.

Matthew 12:35 says the treasure that is in a man determines what happens on the outside. If your heart is filled with good things, good things will be manifested in your life. But if your heart is filled with worldly, ungodly treasure, the same comes forth in your life. Whatever treasure you possess on the inside is what will eventually be seen on the outside. How does this tie into responsibility and life management? We are responsible for the seeds we sow into our hearts, which will ultimately determine the outcome in our lives. In order to see change take place, we must plant the seed of God's Word in our spirits, because it has the power to transform us from the inside out.

The spirit of man, or the heart of man, is the core of our existence. Therefore, how we tend to this part of ourselves really determines our destiny. There are five things we must do to properly manage our spiritual lives.

Properly manage your prayer time. We must be people who are connected to God, and in order to have daily contact with Him, prayer must be at the top of the to-do list. We renew our spirits every day in the presence of God through prayer and personal fellowship time with Him.

When I spend time with God early in the morning, praying, reading the Word, and singing spiritual songs to Him, it refreshes me on the inside. I feel that much more confident to conquer anything that comes my way because of the supercharge I receive during my prayer time with the Lord. Keep in mind that prayer is a dialogue, not a monologue. This simply means that it is just as important that you allow God to speak to you as it is for you to talk to Him. He has things He wants to share with you that will renew your inner man and help you get clear direction in life. Be sure you do not neglect this important aspect of your prayer time with the Lord.

Guard your heart. Your heart is like fertile soil that will produce whatever is planted in it. I liken it to a garden. If you plant the right seeds, you will reap a desirable harvest. By the same token, you have to make sure you do not allow any "weeds" into your heart-garden. What are you allowing into your heart on a daily basis? Are you looking at, listening to, and talking about worldly things that pollute your spirit and produce bad fruit? Or are you keeping your eyes, ears, and mouth in line with God's Word, producing the fruit of the Spirit? The issues of your life flow out of your heart, so keep it protected from ungodly influences.

Guard your relationships. The people we hang out with have the potential to influence us, which is why the Word instructs us to avoid having relationships with people whose lifestyles, morals, and values do not reflect God's standards. This is not to say you should not walk in love toward everyone. But we should not have close fellowship with those whom we are not spiritually compatible. When we do not properly manage our relationships, we can be affected negatively by them. We are responsible for our relationship choices.

Take responsibility for your Word intake. Just as we must eat food to sustain our physical bodies, we also have to feed our spirits the proper diet, which only comes from the Word of God. We must fortify our spirits daily with nourishment from the Word of God.

We are either going to develop thinking that lines up with the Word, or we are going to think like the world. There are no in-betweens. Both of these mind-sets come through the vehicle of words and images. Words from the world determine the way we think, and words from the Word of God also determine our mind-set. So our thought life is determined by what we feed our minds. And the amount of time spent in the Word in order to feed our spirits will be reflected in what comes out of our mouths. Unfortunately, God will not force us to sit down, open the Bible, and read and meditate on the Scriptures. How much time we spend in the Word is solely our responsibility.

Take responsibility for your praise and worship time. Both praise and worship should be a way of life, not just something we do when we come to church on Sundays. Praising God is not some sort of religious exercise, and worship is not singing a slow song to God. Praise is an expression of our appreciation for who God is. It positions us to hear from Him. Worship is obedience to God's instructions to us. It is born out of the intimate relationship we have with Him.

Praise is not limited to church meetings. In fact, you can open your mouth and praise God anywhere! Declare all the wonderful things He has done, and thank Him! Praise Him for who He is in your life. Singing, dancing, clapping your hands, and shouting praises to God paralyze the enemy and release the power of God into your situation. Take time out of your day specifically for praising God, and pay attention to what you hear in your spirit as a result. Worship Him by following through on whatever He tells you to do.

In addition to taking responsibility in our lives, there are four more Rs I want to talk about.

The Second R: Rethinking What You Believe

I mentioned before that we have all been indoctrinated with beliefs and mind-sets that contradict the Word of God. Change cannot take place if we do not critically evaluate what we believe and why we believe it. For example, if sexual lust is an issue in your life, you must start to look at what has determined this mind-set. What are you letting into your spirit that condones this behavior?

When you discover a certain behavior is wrong according to God's Word, you can now make a decision to replace the old belief with the truth. Locate what the Word of God says about it and stick to the truth rather than believe the lie.

The Third R: Rejecting Your Old Ways

This one is often the most challenging because it entails turning away from those things that are pleasurable and enjoyable. The world says living holy is boring and that we somehow miss out when we follow Jesus Christ. But in reality, the only things we miss out on by obeying God are the turmoil and negative consequences of sin and disobedience. I don't mind missing out on those.

God will not force you to let go of your old ways. It ultimately comes down to a personal decision to resist acting on the urges that have been dominating your life. Once you make that choice, you have won half the battle. The good news is, God will help you if you really want to be free.

Spiritual maturity is not determined by how many years you have been saved, or how long you have been a member of your church. It is determined by the decisions you consistently make, and whether those decisions line up with the Word. When we are faced with difficult situations, how we apply the Word to those situations determines our level of maturity. Our decisions also indicate how we are growing in a particular area.

The Fourth R: Review Your New Way of Thinking

Change is predicated on our continually considering and reflecting on the new concepts we are putting in our minds. Each day it is important to take time to go over these principles again and again, continually keeping them before our eyes and in our ears. It will be harder to fall back into old mind-sets when we keep renewing our minds with the truth and reviewing the new information we are taking in.

The Fifth R: Resound Your Thoughts Out Loud

Resounding our thoughts out loud simply means speaking them. This is our confession of faith, and it helps to establish our hearts in the truth of God's Word. Romans 10:10 says, "For with the heart man believeth unto righteousness; and with the mouth confession is made unto salvation." Our confession of God's Word is what activates our salvation, which includes getting our minds back to a place of peace, wholeness, and unity with God. Every time you say the Word, you are hearing it and it is being deposited in your heart. It is also through confession that you are able to cast down ungodly thoughts that try to invade your mind.

Words produce thoughts, so it makes sense that you can change your dominant thought patterns by changing the way you talk. Instead of repeating how defeated and messed up your life is, speak where you want to be and who you want to become. Even though you may not exactly be there yet, if you keep speaking what you want to see in your life, it will eventually become a reality.

If you struggle with a certain behavior or addiction, instead of only picturing yourself free from it, declare out loud, "I have been set free and delivered from addiction. I am prospering in my spirit, soul, and body. I am no longer entangled in those old habits." When you get your mouth involved in the process of change, it accelerates the results.

It is never too late to overcome whatever you may be facing right now. Addictions, bad habits, and wrong mind-sets cannot remain in your life when confronted with the Word of God. It may look like a messy situation, but God is an expert at turning messes into masterpieces! You don't have to be defeated by the devil for a moment. You may have to cry through the process, but continually declare and see yourself coming out. You are changing! Release your faith in the power of God's Word to transform you from the inside out. You are victorious!

NOTES

Introduction

1. James Strong, *New Strong's Exhaustive Concordance of the Bible* (Nashville, TN: Thomas Nelson Publishers, 1996).

Chapter 7

1. The Barna Group, "New Marriage and Divorce Statistics Released," 31 March 2008, http://www.barna.org/barna-update/article/15-family kids/42-new-marriage-and-divorce-statistics-released.

Chapter 9

1. Dr. Creflo A. Dollar and Taffi L. Dollar, *The Successful Family* (Atlanta: Creflo Dollar Ministries, 2004).

Chapter 11

1. http://www.nimh.nih.gov/health/publications/the-numbers-count -mental-disorders-in-america/index.shtml.

Chapter 14

1. *Merriam-Webster's Collegiate Dictionary*, 11th ed. (Springfield, MA: 2006), 259.

Chapter 17

1. http://www.hypertensionhelp.net/stress-and-high-blood-pressure .html; http://www.medicinenet.com/anxiety/symptoms.htm

2. http://psychcentral.com/lib/2006/stress-a-cause-of-cancer/all/1/; http://www.stressrelatedillness.com/stress-and-hypertension.html

Chapter 20

1. *Merriam-Webster's*, 1128.